JAMES C. COBB

BIG

GREEN

CIRCLES

IN THE

DESERT

My Work on the Kufrah-Sarir
Agricultural Project in Libya

Big Green Circles in the Desert

My Work on the Kufrah-Sarir Agricultural Project in Libya

James C. Cobb

CITI OF
BOOKS

CITIOFBOOKS, INC.
3736 Eubank NE Suite A1
Albuquerque, NM 87111-3579
www.citiofbooks.com
Hotline: 1 (877) 389-2759
Fax: 1 (505) 930-7244

Ordering Information:
Quantity sales. Special discounts are available on quantity purchases by corporations, associations, and others. For details, contact the publisher at the address above.

Printed in the United States of America.

ISBN-13:	Softcover	979-8-89391-977-6
	eBook	979-8-89391-979-0
	Hardback	979-8-89391-978-3

Library of Congress Control Number: 2025921282

This book is dedicated to my wife Linda Cobb who waited for me while I had my adventures and misadventures in the Middle East. She kept up a constant stream of letters and care packages. I can't express enough how lucky I am that she didn't find someone else while I was gone and agreed to marry me when I got home. She also put up with my other work-related lengthy absences when I worked in Indonesia and China. We've had a wonderful 44 years together and hope for many more.

Contents

Preface

Writing this book has been on my mind for some time so I'm happy to have it now done. I was offered a job to work in the Middle East when I was finishing a master's degree and lucky things turned out well for me. The experiences I describe in this book were so far from the expected for the life I had been living that they have stayed with me. Working in the Middle East was like I had a small window into international events. Some of the characters I encountered grew in reputation after I returned home, and the wars and violence rose to bigger and more deadly levels. The project I worked on was new and innovative; successful for several decades growing large green circles of alfalfa in the Sahara Desert. These green circles were a frequent target for photographs for space shuttle astronauts because the contract between the barren desert sand and the bright green circles was so stark. In the 1980s, Col. Qaddafi announced his, "Great Manmade River Project," and a giant pipeline was constructed to transfer water from the wells in the desert to the coastal cities. This pipeline was denounced in the news as a ploy for military purposes that could conceal movements of military equipment. In writing this I'm also thinking back on our family friend who in the 1950s and 60s worked for the CIA in Beirut to thwart the notorious Soviet spy Kim Philby, was murdered by the KGB because of his efforts. Going to Beirut sent a chill through my family.

I grew a great deal personally during this time dealing with people and events I could never have imagined would cross my path or me theirs. These experiences played an important role in my career after the work in the desert. In the desert, I had to be up to the job because there was no backup. I had to get the work done in the field despite any obstacles.

I had to get along with people of different backgrounds and cultures. One of the personal lessons I came away with was that people aren't so different even when their governments are at odds with each other or may even be enemies. Most of the people I encountered were helpful, friendly, and capable, but not all. Some were incompetent, arrogant, and difficult, and in their position because of political connections or just the fact of being available. Working closely with all these people was a learning experience for me.

I saved diaries, field notebooks, letters, Kodachrome slides, and the geophysical logs I ran. It took a year to convert the slides to digital format and run them through Photoshop® to bring back their original color. While any errors in my narrative are my own, some of what I relate came from people who I believed knew names, places, and events, etc. and I relied upon their knowledge. Spellings of place names being translated from Arabic are not always uniform from one source to another so there may be minor differences in spelling. Picking illustrations took time because I had so many to sort through. I hope this book gives readers a look through my small window, which I had for two years, on events in a tumultuous and interesting part of the world.

Chapter 1

Job Offer for Beirut

O n July 7, 1974, at about 10:30 p.m. just after twilight turned to night, I was asking myself, *"will I get out of this alive."* I was lost in the Sahara Desert with a driver who didn't speak English; without a map, water, or food. Of course, there's a story behind this memorable time plus others, that I am telling in this book. In 1973, I was finishing a master's degree in geology while my friends were married and beginning their professional careers. I was slower than some of my friends because I changed majors, took five years for my bachelor's degree, and was drafted in 1970 that took another year. My future was just beginning but I didn't know what that would be. Out of the blue, John Foster offered me a job with Foster and Associates, his geophysical company in Beirut, Lebanon. This was totally unexpected, and I had to get out my atlas and find Beirut and Libya.

Chapter 2

Beirut in the 1970s

The Middle East in the 1970s was a hot bed of wars and hijackings but the extent of the violence had not reached the levels exhibited by Al-Qaeda, ISIS, Hezbollah, Hamas, and the Taliban in recent times. The violence then was not generally directed at everyday people, it was targeted at groups who fought each other. Hijackers let passengers deplane before blowing up airplanes which is not to say lethal bombings and assassinations weren't being carried out, but people carried on somewhat normal lives except when violence erupted. The banks and shops closed, and people stayed off the streets. In 1973 the Arab oil embargo was started by the Organization of Petroleum Exporting Countries (OPEC) in retaliation for the U.S. re-supplying weapons to the Israeli military following the Yom Kippur War (1973). This would lead to an energy crisis in the U.S. that President Carter would equate to the "moral equivalent of war," soaring gas prices and long lines at filling stations. Unbeknownst to me at the time, it would eventually point me to fossil energy for a career following my work in the Middle East.

I knew a little about Beirut because a high school classmate of my parents lived in Beirut in the 1950s and 60s. Beirut's reputation for international intrigues stemmed from cold war rivalries between Soviet spies and the West, Muslims fighting Christians, and Palestinians fighting Israelis. Stories about our friend James Barracks being a CIA agent in Beirut were talked about in hushed tones among my parents and their friends who knew him in high school. James' parents and my grandparents were best friends, so information was passed in family circles about things he had done although recent books tell far more sinister versions than what his parents ever talked about. James was from Urbana, Illinois; attended Yale at the time the CIA was conceived; in Army intelligence in Japan in WWII; and then with an alibi as a journalist was sent to Beirut to track down Kim Philby one of the West's most infamous double agents. As an aside to this story, James while on assignment for military intelligence when Japan surrendered in WW II, acquired the largest collection of Japanese Imperial decorations. I inherited this collection which is a story for another book. Philby defected to the Soviet Union in 1963 despite James', the CIA and MI 6's efforts to prevent it. Books written in the 1980s and 90s described the high tensions and intrigues surrounding those events including the fact that in retaliation for James' attempts to thwart Philby, once in Moscow, he ordered James murdered by the KGB on Christmas day 1964. It took a year for US authorities to recover his body and to return it to Urbana. I attended his funeral with my parents in Urbana.

James came to Decatur to visit my parents when on leave from Beirut. When I was in grade school, he brought my brother and me, ivory handled Arabian daggers, an Arabian riding crop, a leopard skin, and two large snake skins. The crop handle concealed a dagger which we thought was really cool. We listened to stories about living in royal palaces in Saudi Arabia and Jordan and being friends with King Saud and King Hussein. He had hunted leopards with King Husain, and escorted members of the Saudi royal family to New York for medical procedures. To me he was a bigger than life figure like *Lawrence of Arabia* with great adventures to his credit. My 25-year-old brain thought big adventures were waiting for me in the Middle East despite the dangers.

With this background on my mind, and John Foster's confidence for the geology work we were going to do, I accepted the offer of $25,000 per year with my living and travel expenses paid. That was considered a good salary for the time. Foster and Associates had a contract to do geologic work for the Kufrah-Sarir Agricultural Project. I was hired to be a field geologist for the project. John Foster had previously worked at the Illinois State Geological Survey (ISGS) and was well known by the staff at the survey. The ISGS director, Bob Bergstrom, who I admired, and John Foster had worked consulting jobs together in the Middle East lending credibility for the offer he was making to me. Foster met me at the ISGS as a student assistant in a temporary position.

My geology degree and electronics repair school I had in the Army fit the requirements for the job. I had to get help from my Congressman Ed Madigan to get a leave of absence from the Illinois National Guard. The job would be to interpret the geology, make geophysical logs of the water wells, and recommend designs for the well casings. The Army electronic repair school was important because there would be inevitable equipment failures that had to be fixed in the field. This was going to be a tall order in a location 500 miles into the Sahara Desert far from access to support. But I was taking a big step for a lifetime career in geology and looked forward to it and downplayed in my own mind the risks I would be taking.

Chapter 3

My Experiences in Beirut

My parents drove me to Chicago O'Hare for the Lufthansa flight to Beirut by way of Frankfurt and Ankara in June 1974. Beirut is at the eastern end of the Mediterranean Sea with beaches, yacht clubs, snowcapped mountains, and ski resorts close by. The climate was great. I was told that there were twenty officially recognized religious sects. Lebanon had power sharing between Christians and Muslims in the constitution. The city was divided into religious and ethnic sections for Muslims, Christians, and other ethnic groups. There was a so-called green line that separated Muslims from Christians. Beirut was commonly referred to as the "Paris of the Middle East." It was more western and cosmopolitan than other Middle Eastern cities. It was the vacation destination for people in the Arab world because it had a large variety of entertainment options including beaches, snow skiing, casinos, western-style restaurants, bars, and nightclubs. People from conservative Muslim countries could indulge in western "excesses" with no constraints. The variety of dress and costumes you could see on the streets was amazing. Beirut was a popular fun place to be in 1974 while at the same time dangerous with outbreaks of violence and groups fighting each other and threats of Israel bombing.

It had discos that were popular in the U.S., one of the popular nightclubs was the *Crazy Horse Saloon*. The week I arrived; a new Holiday Inn Hotel opened in Beirut featuring a revolving restaurant serving beef

5

flown in daily from Chicago. It did not last. Before I departed in 1975, civil war erupted, the hotel was blown up, and in general the city was caught in increasing violence. Later, fighting between Hezbollah and Israel; and invasions by Israel and Syria, Lebanon and Beirut became casualties of the age old, unrelenting power struggles of the Middle East.

I was met at the airport by John Foster. John and his wife Silvia were good hosts and I stayed with them a couple nights at their apartment then moved to the Riviera Hotel. Fosters lived in an apartment south of the city near the airport and adjacent to Palestinian refugee camps. The apartment was nice, and we did company work there. It was an apartment complex in a middle-class community. The apartment complex was an island within an island of refugee camps on the outskirts of Beirut and controlled by the Palestinian Liberation Organization (PLO). In a postcard I sent to Linda showing the beautiful Beirut seashore on June 29, 1974, I wrote, *"Beirut is a nice place to visit but you wouldn't want to live here because we see armed men and hear gun shots often.* Israeli jets fly over and break the sound barrier with a big boom"

Their third-floor apartment had balconies on all four sides. You could see the Mediterranean Sea and a Lebanese army barracks to the west (see Figure 1), Beirut city to the north, the refugee camps (see Figure 2) and the airport to the east and south. The west facing balcony was pock marked by bullets from the Lebanese army when they exchanged gun fire with the PLO in the refugee camps. In my letter to Linda on June 29, 1974, I wrote, *"Foster's apartment is a box seat to a war, and their balcony has 100 bullet strikes from the Lebanese Army and the PLO."* Occasionally the Lebanese Army would fire at the camps in response to events we knew nothing about. News outlets had the phone number and would call to ask John or Silvia to hang the phone over the balcony so they could record sounds of the gunfire for the news. In 1983, 247 U.S. Marines, who were stationed in Beirut as peacekeepers, were killed in a large explosion by a suicide bomber. To underscore what a troubled place this was, the WW II-vintage battleship New Jersey was sent to waters off Beirut in 1984. It fired its 16-inch guns to neutralize Syrian and Druse firing on Beirut.

From the Riviera Hotel, I walked to our office at 106 Piccadilly Center on Al Hamra Street. It was a nice office in an upscale location. We had frequent visitors to our office by religiously attired representatives both Muslim and Christian soliciting donations. We gave because we could never be certain what the consequences might be if we failed to pay. To re-enforce our fears the English language newspaper carried stories about bombings and assassinations. In 1974, Beirut had modern shopping centers and old-world markets called souks. In the town center, instead of city buses, it had a system of circulating taxis on specified routes that served as city buses. Buses could not have passed through the old narrow streets. You could flag down a taxi and if you stayed on the route you only paid a bus fare but if you asked to go off the route then you would pay taxi fares. It was a good system to get around town, but you needed to negotiate the price before you started. On a rainy morning, I was walking to the office, so I flagged a taxi that delivered me to my destination but was off his regular route. The fare he charged was outrageous because I failed to negotiate the price in advance. I complained in harsh words nearly getting into a physical altercation. I forgot for a moment how the system worked and more importantly where I was. He was reaching into his taxi for a weapon when I came to my senses and quickly gave him the money. Thank goodness it ended peacefully.

Israeli war planes flew over Beirut at what seemed like tree top level. They came in very fast and low often breaking the sound barrier scaring people and causing windows and doors to shake. The sonic booms were loud and strong enough to be felt and startled everyone. The planes turned hard to the west racing to get out over the Mediterranean Sea as fast as they could because tiny ribbons of smoke that were surface to air missiles would sometimes chase after them.

To drive in or out of Foster's apartment, which I did often, I had to pass a PLO checkpoint at the refugee camp with guards armed with AK-47 rifles. They weren't aggressive to us but were usually bored, so they *requested* we get out of our car and sit to talk. We would sit by their open fire, drink strong sugared coffee, and discuss Israeli, Palestinian, and Middle East politics. I was wary and uncomfortable, even scared but never overtly threatened. I could not answer their questions about why America supported Israel or even begin to defend U.S. Middle East policy. I was surprised their English was good. My life had been in central Illinois among cornfields and soybeans about as far away from Middle East strife as one could be but the massacre of the Israeli Olympic team in Munich by PLO terrorists was only two years earlier. That event in particular raised huge sentiments for the Israelis because it captured everyone's attention, including mine, because of the brutality being played out on TV. PLO hijackings and terror attacks had swayed me as well as many Americans to the Israeli side as well as the 1973 Yom Kippur war. My sympathies were with Israel, and I couldn't understand why everyone just couldn't live together peacefully. How little I knew about the situation. The other topics thrown at me I was not familiar with were the British mandate, UN resolution 181 (1947), Israel nation state (1948), Six-Day War (1967), UN resolution 242 (1967), Black September (Jordanian-PLO war in 1971), or the appropriation of Palestinian property during the 1948 fight to gain control of the country and subsequent wars. I knew nothing about the history of the Palestinian people, yet there I was the focus of attention in the middle of the largest PLO refugee camp trying to debate these highly complex issues. They were telling me that the hijackings and terrorist activities were because America and Western nations supported Israel and if I was better informed, I would be sympathetic to the Palestinian cause. In my mind I wasn't ready to accept their claims but the violence playing out against civilians was too much to be sympathetic.

One of the PLO guards at the camp was a young man named Mohammed. I think he liked seeing me when we drove up to the check point so he could talk to me. I was younger and American and willing to talk to him. He spoke English well enough to converse and was curious about America. He wanted to know where I was from so I told him Illinois but that did not register so I said, "Chicago, Al Capone," and made a machine gun motion and sound effects which he immediately caught on. He recognized Al Capone the gangster with a machine gun and the association with Chicago. He came from a family of ten children in Egypt, and he told me some Egyptian families with lots of kids sent their boys to join the PLO fighters. I believe he was "volunteered" because his family was in sympathy with PLO cause or because they were financially rewarded for his service or both. Anti-Israeli sentiments ran deep across the Middle East, and he said his family would have fewer mouths to feed. He asked me on several occasions to help him get to America. I would talk to many people in the Middle East expressing anti-American sentiments but also wanting to go to America for a better life. I've wondered what became of Mohammed considering all the wars and violence after I left there.

The living conditions in the refugee camps were poor with make-shift shacks, tents, and even more permanent housing that they had appropriated. Some you could see were made from pieces of road signs, scraps of corrugated roofing material, canvas, plastic, and wood, whatever could be scavenged. Electricity in the power lines crossing the camps was being pirated. I saw "PLO electricians" in the refugee camps put ladders up to live power lines then cut away insulation to attach wires to carry electricity into the camps. The same was true for water and sewers. The people in the camps had skills in their former lives that were being used to make the camps more livable. The Sabra and Shatila camps became infamous when in 1982, Lebanese Phalanges militia with the cooperation of the Israeli Defense Forces cleared out refugees by force. It was estimated as many as 3,500 people in these camps were murdered, although this number is disputed, those who survived were forced onto boats to Tunisia.

The unfinished apartment open to the sky above the Foster's apartment was being prepared for a missile site to fire at Israeli jets that flew over Beirut. There was a PLO command post in the backyard of the apartment complex. PLO fighters came to the door for a drink of water or to use the toilet. It was strange to see a PLO fighter lay down his rifle to use the toilet or get a drink then say *shukran* which is Arabic for thank you when he left.

An unforgettable event for me was a gun battle between *who knows which warring factions* at a major intersection while I was in a taxi on my way to the airport. Rather than being scared for my safety, I was fascinated that people were shooting at each other across a busy highway. I was more intrigued than scared. Events like this were so unbelievable but not uncommon in Beirut.

Foster's apartment was one floor above a German baron. John arranged for us to visit him for drinks in his apartment. John prepared me beforehand that this would be an experience I would not forget. He told me "Heinz" was German but spoke English, was a friendly fellow, but that we would not ask about his work. So, we walked downstairs and were greeted by Heinz who was handsome, about 70, in great shape, and charming. He ushered us into his apartment making no comments about his decor. I was stunned and taken aback because the entryway was a shrine to Adolf Hitler with portraits, Nazi flags and symbols covering the walls. We sat in his living room, and he served us drinks. We talked about our neighbors, the PLO fighters and refugee camps, and our upcoming work in Libya. He shared a story about his girlfriend riding her bicycle to the apartment and one day it disappeared. He reported this to the PLO command post in the yard of the apartment. The bicycle was returned the next day. Looking into the refugee camps when passing by, there was an appearance of disorder, but apparently there was control although not obvious. Heinz had clout with the PLO perhaps stimming from his German heritage. There were so many things I wanted to ask. I had read novels about Odessa, the organization of former Nazi SS whose purpose was to sustain members hiding around the world. I thought that was just fiction for a good story. Apparently not. Foster told me he believed Heinz was a member of that or a similar organization. He was often away, and there were suspicions he delivered messages and money to former Nazis.

There was another incident that reinforced for me Lebanon was an active war zone. During a dinner party at the Foster's apartment, their live-in housekeeper, a 75-year-old Palestinian woman received word her 80-year-old sister was killed that day in an Israeli bombing raid in southern Lebanon. This woman and her family fled Palestine when the Zionists took control. Her family had been refugees for 27 years. The Palestinian people had lived many generations in Palestine, a place that for millennia experienced violent religious conflict interspersed with times of peace. It was particularly sad and poignant, the killing of this 80-year-old woman who had lived her old age as a refugee, whereas killing of PLO fighters receiving pay back for the atrocities they committed was quite another matter. I learned the exile from Palestine was referred to as the *Nakba* when civil war broke out in 1948. Hundreds of thousands of Palestinians were forcibly driven from their homes and many were killed. Knowing the people involved in tragic event makes it much more personal than reading about it in the newspaper. I was not particularly sympathetic to the PLO fighters, but I did feel the Palestinian people were treated badly. In my free time I took trips to historic places like Tyre, Sidon, Byblos, and Baalbek (see Figures 3, 4, and 5). Places spoken of in the Bible and places fought over by Babylonians, Assyrians, Persians, Phoenicians, Romans, Crusaders, Turks, Muslims, and the Byzantine, Ottoman and British Empires. Baalbek had the largest stone columns every erected and the largest quarried block, the size of a small house, accomplished by the Romans. There were ruins and archeological sites nearly everywhere.

Foster and I prepared for the Libya work. We found a Dodge dealer to buy a four-wheel drive pickup truck to carry the geophysical equipment in Libya. While at the dealership we met two staff members from the Soviet Embassy also purchasing a Dodge pickup and shared a few laughs and Turkish coffee while making our purchases. I was amazed at how cordial people from such different backgrounds could be and how many spoke English. Odd occasions like this were common in Beirut. We took the pickup to a shop that made custom toppers for trucks and had a camper-like topper built for the truck bed. The topper was insulated and air conditioned for the hot desert conditions in Libya.

John Foster introduced me to his Beirut friends and hosted several dinner parties so I could get to know other Americans in Beirut. Foster was a U.S. Air Force B-29 pilot whose plane crashed on a training mission leaving him with a permanent limp. After his crash, he worked for the Air Force on the Minuteman missile program locating underground missile silos in North and South Dakota. On the list of specifications for a missile silo location in the 1950s was that the North Star had to be visible through a ten feet long tube 4 inches in diameter. That always stuck with me. It seemed natural that many of his Beirut friends were pilots. One of John's close friends was a pilot for Jordanian Airlines and flew King Husain. He was landing a Boeing 707-300 in Nigeria when the plane broke through a faulty runway killing 180 of the people on board. The plane was a charter for Nigerians returning from Mecca for the Haj. He and his co-pilot survived but were arrested by the local authorities and accused of causing the crash. They had to be smuggled out of the country.

A bar named the Captains Quarters in Beirut was a meeting place for Americans in Beirut. I was intrigued by the stories, personalities, adventures, and lifestyles of the people I was meeting. But the flip side of all these adventures and high living was people deadening their personal problems with alcohol. Alcohol was a big part of everyday life starting early in the day. I was mentally processing how this expat lifestyle could be fulfilling and sustainable. Finally, it was time to leave for Libya and the field work ahead.

Chapter 4

Arrival in Libya

I knew much of my time would be spent in Libya in the desert but very little about the area where the field work would be done. I knew that Commodore Stephen Decatur had fought America's first war (1801-05) against the Tripoli pirates, I grew up in Decatur, Il, named for Commodore Stephen Decatur. My Dad's ship the USS Weehawken docked in Benghazi in WW II preparing for the invasion of Italy. I knew it was a third world country and mostly desert but didn't really know what third world really meant. I also knew PLO terrorists had recently blown up a Japan Airline 747 in July 1973 at the Benghazi airport. Libya had been in the news since 1969 because dictator Col. Muammar Qaddafi had come to power following a military takeover of the government. On reflection it was not an attractive profile for a country I would be working in. Libya was a backward Muslim country in North Africa formally an Italian colony. Being in the Middle East it had all the political tensions that are common to the region. This included a split government with two capitols, Benghazi and Tripoli, a safe haven for terrorists, and civil turmoil. As I recall this now, it shocks me that I accepted the offer and my parents later ask, "Why didn't we talk him out of going?" I was anxious for the big salary, real-world experience and an adventure. I was motivated to prove something to myself and like many 25-year-olds I felt invincible.

The Middle East Airline flight to Benghazi stopped in Cairo, Egypt. It was cool seeing the Nile River delta and the Great Pyramids of Giza from the air. As we flew west to Benghazi even at 30,000 feet the air outside the plane was tinged red with dust blown up from the Sahara. When the plane landed at the Benghazi airport it was impossible to miss the burned-out wreckage from the hijacked 747 airplane left there for political effect or just neglect. Then on leaving the airport for the city, I could not miss the billboard with pictures of the murders of the Israeli Olympic team from the Munich Olympics who had taken refuge in Libya.

The drive from the airport was long and I was shocked by the reality of being in a third world country with its poor roads, goat herders, litter and plastic bags caught in scraggly brush, and people along the road selling produce. I was picked up at the airport by staff from the Kufrah-Sarir Agricultural Project and dropped off at the Omar Khayyam Hotel, formerly a five-star Hilton Hotel before it was taken over by the government. As I was to learn on many occasions when checking in, a bribe, "baksheesh," to the desk clerk was required before he would even check for room availability. You would put a 20-dinar bill into your passport and pass it to him. It was a very nice hotel that even had a casino on the lower level but that had been closed and the gaming tables covered with sheets. I wrote to Linda, *"The hotel was excellent, one of the best I had ever stayed in,"*

I made many trips to Benghazi and the Omar Khayyam Hotel was a welcome sight. I felt safe and comfortable there and had opportunities to meet other Americans working in Libya. Most of them were in the oil business. To me there was no second-place hotel. I heard stories from other Americans who had miserable experiences at other hotels in Benghazi. On more than one occasion, I arrived with no reservation and was at the mercy of the arrogant desk clerk. I had gotten accustomed to paying him the 20-dinar bribe but then hearing from him there were no rooms available threw me into a panic. I must have looked pathetic to him so he said, "we have a broom closet you can stay in with a roll-a-way bed until a regular room opens up." I said I would take it. The room was not a broom closet because it had a bed, sink and toilet. Some extra furniture was stored there but otherwise it was okay. I was happy to be there. I stayed in it more than once.

I heard the calls to prayer from minarets in Beirut but in Benghazi the volume was louder. There were five calls to prayer each day and the first one was just as first rays of sunlight could be seen. What would have been the Hilton Hotel bar was a coffee shop. Libya had been an Italian colony, so they served expresso, cappuccino, tea, Turkish coffee, Pepsi, Fanta, and fruit drinks. Smoking was a popular social thing. Everyone seemed to smoke British or Egyptian cigarettes and with each one pulled from the pack, all the people at the table would be ceremoniously offered one. The pack would make the rounds of the table.

The hotel dining room was nice and served good food. I learned you must specify bottled water by "with gas" or "sin gas", that is with or without carbonation. Most choose with gas because it was thought to be fresh and untainted and not recycled as the carbonation would presumably be lost if tampered with. That notion was dispelled when we ate at a late hour and being the last patrons of the night saw how the bottles not completely emptied were used to fill the bottles that would be served the next night. Bottle caps were saved to add that authentic touch of opening a fresh bottle. I especially liked Libyan soup. Many of the dishes consisted of mutton and rice with vegetables like squash and eggplant. Breakfasts had eggs and cereal but of course no bacon or ham.

I was in the hotel lobby waiting for a ride to the project office when Libyan soldiers came in and forces each guest in the lobby to sit. They stood in front of each of us so we could not get up. They sealed off the coffee shop, dining room, and elevators. We were not allowed to move. Col. Qaddafi and his entourage came in and went up the elevator to the meeting rooms on the mezzanine level. Once Qaddafi was gone, we could move. Another time, I witnessed from my hotel window Qaddafi giving a speech to a large military contingent across the street from the hotel. It reminded me of a cartoon caricature of a third world dictator then I realized *he was a third world dictator.* I thought the hotel windows might be watched by Qaddafi's secret police, so I didn't take pictures and stayed back from the window while I watched. I certainly didn't want to draw attention to myself. His speech lasted a couple of hours. Often from my hotel room, in the middle of the night, I heard distinctive noises of heavy military vehicles being off-loaded from the harbor and passing the hotel. The exhaust noise from tanks was unmistakable. The Soviet Union was supplying Qaddafi's army with military equipment.

The hotel was near enough to the city's central park that I often walked there just to see the markets and stores. It was routine to have on public display wrecked cars from recent fatal traffic accidents. Deadly traffic accidents were common because Libya had no driver education and little if any traffic law enforcement. The wrecked cars would be roped off and a sign posted telling the body count from that accident. Although gruesome to look at with the blood and gore still visible, it was an attempt to shock drivers into being more careful.

Chapter 5

Kufrah-Sarir Agricultural Project

At the Kufrah-Sarir Agricultural Project headquarters, I was given a desk in an otherwise barren office. It was a very undistinguished looking building like so many others two stories and had almost no furniture or office supplies. The only attempt at decorating was a large portrait of Col. Moammar Qaddafi. I was introduced to an older British man who had spent years in Palestine in the administration until the British pulled out. He became my mentor. He spoke Arabic and was full of knowledge and important advice about working for the project. I relied on him a lot. One of the odd things I remember about the office was that cups of strong sweet Turkish coffee were constantly delivered by street venders. The hot coffee was brewed over charcoal fires on the street and served in water glasses, so I had to learn how to hold one until it cooled off. Since the city water was not safe to drink, I wondered how or if the glasses were washed and what water was used to make the coffee. I don't think I wanted to know the answer. The scalding temperature seemed sufficient to kill harmful bacteria.

The project's objective was to construct 100 water wells 36 inches in diameter, 1,000 feet deep, and cased with fiber glass well casing. High capacity submersible pumps would then be installed and connected to pivot irrigation machines. The circular irrigated fields were to grow alfalfa for feeding sheep. My job was to record the geology of the wells, recommend the casing design to the contractor; prepare a geologic study to estimate the water resources of the area; and oversee the cleaning and testing of the wells before the pivot irrigation machines were installed.

The Kufrah-Sarir water project was important to Col. Muammar Qaddafi and he promoted it as an example of the good he was doing for Libya with his oil revenues. Thanks to the Sarir oil field, Libya had become the largest oil producer in Africa. The discovery of oil in the 1950s also found abundant fresh groundwater in the shallow subsurface. A simple calculation of the potential groundwater resources was enough to encourage a project like the Sarir water project to demonstrate that the groundwater could be used for the good of the people in a country with virtually no surface freshwater, no rivers, and no lakes. The Sarir water project was the first to test this idea. Libya's rise to being Africa's largest petroleum producer could well pay the costs of developing the groundwater for agriculture. The plan for Sarir was to construct large capacity water wells that would be connected to pivot irrigation machines that would irrigate circular fields of alfalfa. The alfalfa would be fed to sheep for mutton and wool. The sheep would be transported to the cities. That was the plan.

All foreign companies working in Libya had to have a Libyan agent. Our agent negotiated our contracts and obtained our permits and visas through the various government bureaucracies. I was told his father had been an official in the government of King Idris but was now in exile. We never knew what he had to do or pay to keep working in Libya. He was educated in England, spoke excellent English, and his appearance was very western. Qaddafi set up local "citizen committees" empowered as watchdogs to check up on businesses and could invite themselves into our private meetings just by showing up. They could not be ignored or turned away. These were uneducated and unsophisticated locals but if ignored or left out of the conversation could cause trouble. Our agent went to great lengths to act welcoming when they showed up. Their principal motivation seemed to be intimidation, smoking his cigarettes and drinking his coffee. I never knew but could guess he paid them "baksheesh" (bribes) as a *thank you* for "*caring about our work.*"

His secretary surprisingly was an American woman who had come to Libya as a representative of the company that sold the pivot irrigation machines. She met and married a petroleum engineer from Utah who was also working in Libya. He was Mormon and there was a group of Mormons in Benghazi working in the oil business. The Mormons met as a group to socialize and hold church services in secret. They seemed to know when other Americans arrived because I was invited to join them for a Christmas celebration. I was impressed by their faithfulness and boldness because being discovered could have resulted in arrest, expulsion, and possibly prison. My parents sent a box with a Christmas gift, a small wooden Hallmark nativity scene. The Libyan customs agents got carried away stealing the goodies; a toothbrush, toothpaste, shampoo, and soap but missed the one thing most meaningful and illegal in Libya. If they had known its meaning, the birth of Jesus Christ, it never would have been allowed to get to me. At worst I could have been arrested for practicing Christianity. I get that nativity scene out for Christmas ever year. It is one of my most valued keepsakes

I was assigned a Land Rover and driver for my own personal use on the project and our geophysical logger would be installed in it. My British friend found a metal shop and we took the Land Rover into the rat maze of roads in Benghazi to a machine shop and ordered two racks to be built in the back of the Land Rover to hold extra jerry cans of gasoline. The Land Rover had an 18-gallon tank, and I estimated it got about 20 miles per gallon. Each rack held two five-gallon jerry cans. That gave 20 extra gallons for the approximately 500-mile trip from Benghazi to Sarir which would surely be enough.

Since all the preparations I could do for my departure were complete, such as they were, I went with friends to the Benghazi French Beach Club for a swim and sun in the Mediterranean Sea. In a letter I wrote to Linda I said, *"I got a sunburn today at the beach, a fine way to begin a trip into the Sahara Desert."* And, *"I've picked up a few words of Arabic so I'm getting along better with the language barrier. I'm nervous about the long drive to the Sarir camp because occasionally workers at the*

Sarir oil field get lost in the desert." I had heard stories that made me nervous about men getting lost in the desert.

Chapter 6

Driving Across the Sahara Desert

My departure for Sarir was scheduled for July 7, 1974. Although we didn't have a map at the time we departed, I drew one from various other sources just for my own use in case I needed it. because it shows roughly the route from Benghazi to Sarir and Kufrah (see Figure 6). The driver picked me up at the hotel at about 10:00 a.m. It was my first time meeting him and he did not speak English. I knew virtually nothing about the drive we were to make from Benghazi to the Sarir camp. All I knew was that we were venturing into the Sahara Desert in the summer, and I had a driver who didn't speak English. My self-preservation instincts kicked in when I noticed we had no water container in the back of our vehicle. I insisted on buying one before leaving Benghazi in case the worst happened, and we became stranded in the desert. I got my point across to the driver by drawing pictures in my notebook, so we stopped at a market and purchased a five-gallon Igloo® water container. I also bought three watermelons and a couple bottles of orange Fanta.

On our way south we passed an abandoned fortress (see Figure 7) and stopped to walk around and stretch our legs. It was fascinating because there were hundreds of spent shells casings and debris like boots and tin ware. It was probably where a WW II battle had taken place, but I had no way to know the history of this abandoned relic.

We headed south to the Sarir camp with the Igloo® container still empty. I was feeling frustrated and anxious. I was surprised when we stopped in Ajdabeya, a town about 150 miles south of Benghazi but not yet in the desert. It was the last city before we ventured into the desert. I was very concerned that we would be transporting an empty water cooler all the way to Sarir, but we finally filled it at a bottling plant in the town. That was very satisfying for me. I was now starting to have more trust in the driver that he might know more than I thought he did. I then figured out this was his hometown, and he took me on a brief tour first to the bunker used by German General Erwin Rommel during the North African campaign in WWII, then a second stop at a memorial in honor of a Libyan martyr. The martyr had led a revolt against the Italians and was hung at that very spot. The wooden scaffold was still there as a reminder of his sacrifice.

Next, we parked in front of a private residence, and he made gestures for me to wait in the vehicle while he went inside (see Figure 8). I stayed in the Land Rover for about 15 minutes not knowing why we had stopped. I was invited in and immediately smelled food cooking and was introduced to two men. I assumed these men were possibly a father and brother. The interior was clean but sparsely furnished. The floors were terrazzo with rugs. We sat on cushions on the floor. I was offered Egyptian cigarettes and Turkish coffee. I declined the cigarettes but accepted the sweet coffee.

A carved wooden partition separated the living room where we were from the kitchen. I could hear kitchen noises and smell the cooking and heard giggling from behind the partition. Occasionally I could see eyes looking through the partition at me. The females of the household not being allowed to be in the presence of a male not their relative while uncovered were preparing the food and sneaking looks at me.

The food came out on a large metal platter placed on the floor between us containing rice, chicken and squash covered in a sauce, and pita bread. We used the bread to snatch up the food by hand. There were no utensils, but the food was good, and I caught on quickly to eating with one hand. I knew enough to eat with my right hand because to extend my left hand would not have been good. You only eat with your right hand. When we were finished eating, the three men became engrossed in conversation and smoked strong cigarettes that I again declined. I felt out-of-place and uncomfortable not just because I was unable to communicate but because my hosts didn't try to make me feel welcome. This was Libya.

It was late afternoon when we started driving but in June days are long so we still had hours of daylight which should have been enough time to cover the remaining 300 miles. When the paved road ended (see Figure 9), we were in desert sand on the Italian Road that had iron markers standing 8 feet high and spaced one kilometer apart. Each one was adorned with a crown on top showing the compass directions and the distance in kilometers north to Benghazi and south to Al Jawf-Kufrah. I was so impressed by the kilometer markers I drew a picture of one in my field notebook (see Figure 10).

Vegetation was very sparse as we left Benghazi driving south. When we left the paved road onto the desert sand, only sand formed the landscape as far as the eye could see. Something I didn't expect was the optical illusions I got because of the intense sun shining on desert sand and nothing for scale, as I looked at the sand in front of us. A drink can lying in our path in the distance appeared as if it could be a 55-gallon drum but as we got close, it was obviously only a 12 oz. drink can. With no trees or vegetation of any kind, no cars or trucks, nothing for scale something as small as a drink can was difficult to recognize for what it really was. The notion of the desert playing tricks on you is true and is how people can become disoriented. The heat rising from the surface caused a wavy affect that looked like wet spots in the distance but of course they were merely a mirage. Another thing that was surprising was the debris scattered along the road; war debris, camel skeletons, and discarded vehicle parts. Lots of mummified camel skeletons.

It was frustrating not being able to talk to the driver, so I never had confidence he knew much about where we were going or the progress we were making. I was worried we were not making good time and might have to spend the night in the desert. There were occasional heavy trucks coming north towards us. These were oil industry trucks returning to Benghazi for oil field supplies. There was no defined road only tracks and ruts running north-south but several miles wide. When a vehicle coming north appeared in the distance, it would veer over to get close enough to see the other driver up close by the time they passed. It must be human curiosity to want to see who else is out in this desolate place.

Our first mishap was losing our water. The water cooler flew out the back of the Land Rover when we ran over a pipeline buried just beneath the sand but not obvious enough to be seen before it was too late. It was like hitting a speedbump at 50 miles per hour. When we hit the pipeline, the vehicle bucked violently, and the five-gallon cooler was ejected out the back. The lid popped off and the water ran out before we could stop and recover the cooler. It was a shock, and I was scared knowing we had no water.

The next thing that happened was we lost track of the mile markers on the road. The road markers might have been knocked down and we were unknowingly veering off course to the east. We were no longer on the "marked" road and no longer on the route to the Sarir camp and didn't know it. We had not seen a road marker in a long time or any vehicles coming north or even the ruts and tracks that looked like a highly trafficked road. I had no idea what my driver was thinking because we could not communicate. We had only two bottles of orange Fanta plus three watermelons as our Igloo® water container was now empty and daylight was fading (see Figure 11). My imagination began playing with me forming pictures in my mind of people crawling in the sand toward mirages they never get to dying of thirst; images I had seen in movies. By this time, I knew we would not get to the camp before dark. It was getting cold, and I was scared. I was learning that desert cold was worse than desert heat.

As it became dark, we took turns climbing onto the hood of the Land Rover to look for lights with binoculars that I had brought. I suspected my driver's backup plan was to get to the vicinity of the Sarir camp and look for lights from the drill rigs with 80 feet tall masts that were lit at night. He was counting on spotting a rig that would show us the way to the camp. Even standing on the hood of the vehicle with binoculars we could see nothing. We were lost in the vast Sahara Desert! We drove in the darkness, literally driving blind for about an hour until we finally saw a light and drove to it. It was an outpost for the Libyan army put there to check permits (see Figure 12) required to enter the Sarir Oil Field. There was a lone soldier manning the outpost. My driver and I had the required permits that allowed us to be in this area. The good news was we were in the Sarir Oil Field, but the bad news was we had strayed far off course and we were a long way from the Sarir agricultural project camp. The soldier at this outpost allowed us to stay at his camp for the night. I got the idea from my driver he would help us get to our camp the next day. I thought to myself, *"Why did I get myself into this, I haven't even started my work yet?"*

That night under the stars the three of us watched satellites and airplanes passing over but the real treat was to see the Milky Way so vividly. It's impossible to describe how much you can see in the night sky when you are far from city lights, clouds, and humidity. I pulled out my compass to show my companions how it pointed to the North Star. I was pretty sure they had never used a compass. We cut up the melons I had purchased in Benghazi. I had my Boy Scout knife to do the cutting and the soldier had a pan for us to eat out of. After our second melon was cut and eaten, I happened to notice he was taking the pan with the melon rinds to feed his camel. We were eating out of the same pan as the camel. I did the cutting for the third melon but passed on eating any.

The outpost consisted of a small shack not much bigger than an outhouse, a canvas tent, a vehicle, and a camel. I was offered the tent for sleeping. It was totally empty, no cot, no anything, empty. My driver slept in the Land Rover which was not big enough to stretch out in. It was getting cold and I had a hooded sweatshirt that I put on. As I carved out a sleeping spot in the sand, I noticed large things moving in the sand. My flashlight beam illuminated large spiders moving in the sand. These spiders were big and freaked me out. I had no idea how dangerous they were or if they posed a threat of biting me in the night. I had been warned about deadly scorpions in the Sahara but had not heard about these spiders. I went to the tool box in the Land Rover and got out electrical tape and taped my pant legs, shirt cuffs, and neck to keep the spiders out as best as I could. With my hoodie drawstrings pulled as tight as possible, I only had a small amount of skin exposed. By this time, it was very late so only a few hours left before sunrise. Fortunately, the spiders left me alone. I have since investigated Sahara sand spiders and they are poisonous. I was lucky.

At sunrise we fueled the Land Rover with our jerry can and started on our way. The soldier took over driving so three of us crowded into the front seat. I thought we must be close because we had driven a lot the previous day and used two of the four jerry cans of gasoline. We had 15 gallons in our tank and only one remaining jerry can. We drove until about 2:00 p.m. and after putting our last five gallons in, we came to a permanent-looking camp. I thought this must be our camp, but it wasn't! It was an oil field camp. Our new guide got it wrong. He took us to the oil field camp not the Sarir agricultural project camp.

A conversation went on among my driver, the guide and the camp personnel. The Sarir agricultural project camp was still 80 miles off. I was really discouraged. The good news was the oil drillers could get us there. Apparently because of their work schedule, we were invited to stay the night, refuel, and fill up the water cooler which I securely tied down, but couldn't leave until the next morning. We ate real food and were offered a bunk for the night. Halleluiah no spiders! I ate well and slept well. The conditions at this camp were a huge improvement over the previous night. But again no one spoke English.

The next morning, we ate a good breakfast and headed out. The desert soldier was driving my Land Rover and we were following a Land Rover driven by oil camp personnel. After about three hours of driving we saw a white Land Rover and drove to meet it. It was from the Sarir water camp with people out looking for us. The oil field personnel turned back to their camp with our thanks. The white Land Rover had Geotehnika personal and Frederick Arthur Rawlings III who was my colleague from Foster and Associates. We were two days overdue and the camp was worried about what happened to us. I found out later we had veered far off course to the east and ran into the Sarir oil field but that mistake also saved our lives because if we had missed the oil field then we would have been lost with little chance anyone would have found us; at least in time to do us any good. Again, I was lucky.

The drama was not over because Rawlings automatically got in the driver's seat behind the wheel. He believed himself to be the senior person and this was a F&A vehicle, so he was entitled to drive. The desert soldier refused to hand over the keys, so I was in the middle and Rawlings got into the passenger seat. My driver climbed into the back of the Land Rover. As we headed to the camp at high speed our vehicle swayed sharply from side to side and bucked violently as we crossed over deep ruts caused by heavy equipment. Rawlings became upset and demanded the soldier stop and turn the driving over to him. When he did not, Rawlings turned the ignition off and removed the key. At that point the soldier drew his pistol waving it in front of my face because I was sitting in the middle. Rawlings handed the keys back de-escalating the rising tensions, so we proceeded to the camp.

The drive from Benghazi to Sarir to this point had been very stressful but now things seemed out of control. What was supposed to be a routine one-day drive turned out to be a miserable two-and-a-half-day ordeal ending with a confrontation between two outraged people who couldn't communicate with each other. The drama was not over because the offended soldier now highly agitated began making demands for food and supplies from the Sarir camp to be taken back to his outpost. Before he left the camp, he came to my trailer where I was unpacking. Using angry words and gestures he demanded my compass and knife that I had used the night at his outpost. I had no choice but to hand them over to him. Geotehnika staff from the camp drove him back to his station and I was happy to see him go. However, I was now nervous because of the outburst by Frederick Arthur Rawlings III and worried about his mental stability because I was going to be working with him and sharing a room with him. Life at the Sarir camp could be a challenge. I wrote in a letter to Linda, *"Frederick Arthur Rawlings III is very British, stuffy, a know-it-all, non-stop talker, physically fit, about 60, married a new wife five years ago, and spent the last 30 years working jobs in Africa and Arabia."* This was my welcome to the Sarir camp.

Chapter 7

Sarir Camp

While I was getting oriented for work on the project in Benghazi, the Sarir camp was being built by Geotehnika, a Yugoslavian drilling company (see Figure 13). Geotehnika's job was to provide housing, dining facilities, water and waste facilities, infirmary, laundry, house cleaning, vehicle maintenance, office facilities, and of course operate the three drill rigs. The camp had its own power plant and fresh water, so all the trailers had electricity, showers, toilets and air conditioners. The trailers were cleaned daily, and sheets changed weekly. We had free laundry service. The conditions were pretty good for being in such a harsh environment. Geotehnika even made a fountain in the center of the living quarters with flowing water and green plants. I was sharing a trailer with Rawlings and wrote to Linda, *"I'm about to go crazy having to put up with Frederick Arthur Rawlings III, I've about reached my limit."* Frederick spoke often about his life in British Northern Rhodesia playing bridge with society people and government officials. He was arrogant and an insufferable snob.

An interesting aspect of the camp was that it was partitioned between the Yugoslavian enclave and the Pakistani/laborer enclave. Each enclave had 8 house trailers capable of housing four or more people. So, the Yugoslavian personnel, project advisors like me, and guests lived in one part of the camp while the Pakistanis and laborers lived in another.

The dining and laundry facilities were in the middle of the camp, but the Pakistanis and laborers ate in a separate dining area.

Geotehnika's previous job was drilling water wells in Kenya 4,000 miles to the south. Geotehnika was a highly mobile operation capable of moving their entire operation by overland caravan (see Figure 14). This caravan had travelled across one-third of Africa south to north with three large Failing 5000 drill rigs plus all their equipment and a crew of 40. That was an amazing feat.

The company headquarters was in Zagreb, Yugoslavia (see Figure 15) but the workers were from several places in Yugoslavia like Serbia, Croatia, Kosovo, and Bosnia. I had never heard those names before. I caught comments being made that most of the Yugoslavians were Christian, but some were Muslim. I detected subtle discrimination based on ethnicity and religion. That was prophetic considering the bloody civil war and genocide that ensued in the 1990s with the civil war, genocide, and breakup of Yugoslavia. However, camp life in 1974 was very harmonious.

Geotehnika was responsible for drilling wells, installing well casing, submersible pumps, electrical power, and pivot irrigators. Yugoslavians were the rig bosses, and their tool pushers were Pakistanis who operated the rigs. Roughnecks, who were Sudanese and Chadians were at the bottom of the pecking order and did the dirtiest jobs. They had the darkest skin that I had ever seen. Their skin tone was nearly purple. They did dangerous jobs like coupling and uncoupling drill pipes; pulling pipe; climbing the mast to untangle cables; mixing the drill mud; and cleaning the equipment. There was a hierarchy of nationalities and cultures. I noticed that none of the Libyans did any of the manual labor and their participation in planning, analyzing, and discussing geology and hydrology was minimal. The project relied on foreign workers and advisors.

Running the geophysical logs was a challenge because I had never done that before in any of my previous jobs. I was learning on the job. I was required by contract to teach the Libyan geologists how to do the jobs I was doing. When the first well was ready, I took the logger out to the well and set up to run logs. My Libyan counterparts were hanging all over me and the tools wanting to turn dials and operate the equipment. I had been expecting this so I spent several nights by myself making dry runs so at least I could operate the equipment once the pressure was on. The operating manuals were good, and I ran all the logs successfully even with an over eager audience. They never knew it was my first-time operating the geophysical logger. Except for drilling, logging the wells was one of the more interesting things going on at the camp that drew a big audience. Many times, I had six or seven people crowding around to see the logging operation except at night when I was alone. I liked logging at night.

Meanwhile Frederick Arthur Rawlings III stayed close to the trailer and his bed, did no actual work, and constantly harassed the camp staff about picayune things that bothered him which was pretty much everything. He wore custom tailored desert attire and strutted about like the British colonial bureaucrat that he had been and talked in the same manner. Frederick Arthur Rawlings III succeeded in offending everyone because of his arrogant manner and unreasonable requests. Our air conditioner mysteriously broke, sand got into his bed sheets, then when he went out of the country for a break to Malta, his visa was revoked, and he could not re-enter Libya. Hooray, the trailer was all mine, I could do the work and had no problems with any of the camp personnel and was glad he was not returning. I was happy.

Miraculously my air conditioner was fixed, and the room had no sand in it. I passed the word that Frederick Arthur Rawlings III's clothes would be available; first come first serve. There was soon a que at my trailer and so I handed out his clothes. I'll never forget days later making my rounds of the drill rigs seeing roughnecks wearing his custom-tailored shorts and shirts mixing mud. That made me smile. I never saw nor heard from him again. He was gone and I didn't have him in my way anymore and everything was harmonious for me at Sarir.

Life at Sarir camp became a routine. I got to know most of the Yugoslavians because my trailer was in their compound. We sat out at night and talked as best we could because of the language barrier, played or watched games of chess, and listened to BBC world news on a shortwave radio. I spent the days driving from rig to rig, analyzing samples, assembling geologic data and interpreting well logs. I started to receive mail and packages from home from Linda and my parents. Linda sent me tapes, food and pictures. In a letter to her I wrote, *"we drive out to the sand dunes for fun and see how far up the back side we can go and driving in the desert was like being at sea; out of sight of land, rocking from side to side, and nothing on the horizon."* That's what we did for fun. Occasionally we heard reports of people lost in the desert, so we had to be careful and track carefully our locations with respect to the Sarir camp. Certainly, none of us wanted to get lost in the desert.

Being the only American and having given away Frederick Arthur Rawlings III's clothes to the workers, I was getting to be known in the camp. After dinner people started coming to my trailer to ask for favors that were mostly about writing letters to the American Embassy in Tripoli asking for visas to go to the US. There were nights when two or three people needed letters written in English. I wrote some letters to American universities asking for applications for admission. The funniest requests came from the Libyans who wanted male sex lotions they had seen in ads in Playboy magazines that had been smuggled into the country. Apparently, they were worried about their performance with their wives when at home.

At the end of Ramadan in 1974, I was honored by being made a Pakistani for the day. I was invited to the Pakistani camp for the feast of Eid that celebrates the end of fasting for the Islamic holy month of Ramadan. They even provided me a Pakistani outfit to wear, the huge drawstring pants and the tunic-type shirt. I got along well with these guys because they were operating the drill rigs and I worked with them every day. I was reminded that although countries and governments could be at odds, even war, ordinary people could be respectful of each other and even friends. Most of the people I encountered in Libya were kind to me. Diplomatic relations between Libya and the US got so bad in 1974-5, that Libya severed ties and demanded the closing of the

American Embassy. Americans were told to leave Libya and I believed I that I would be leaving too. While the Embassy did close, American workers were asked privately to stay because it became obvious that jobs especially in the oil fields could not be done without Americans. I was asked to stay. I was even asked to quit F & A and work directly for the Libyan Water Authority. I did not take them up on that offer.

I was meeting John Foster in Benghazi during this troubled time. The American consulate office in Benghazi was sacked and burned while across the street people were calmly drinking coffee and smoking in an outdoor café. It was a staged *spontaneous* event by the government. The American Embassy in Tripoli was also burned. I couldn't help but draw a comparison to the events in 2012 that took the lives of the ambassador and three other Americans. My experience with the bogus mob in Benghazi in 1975, made me angry when our Secretary of State and UN Ambassador both lied repeatedly on national news that a mob reacting to a video burned the counselor office and killed Ambassador Chris Stevens and three Americans. It's obvious to me some of our government leaders have no shame and will lie to maintain their public image.

Linda sent me letters and care packages. In one of these boxes, there was a cassette tape recording of Richard Nixon resigning the presidency. The tape also had Maria Muldauer singing, "Midnight at the Oasis." The box contained crumpled aluminum foil and Saran wrap; empty wrappers from baked goodies left in the nearly empty box. The Libyan customs agents had eaten my goodies. I do remember discussing Nixon's resignation with my colleagues who were vocal about how weak America was if the president could be forced from office without violence and civil war. There was no way I could convince them that what was happening in America showed our strength. America's system of government was working to keep the people safe from dictators like Qaddafi and his ilk that plagued Muslim countries. It was obvious the Libyans, Yugoslavians, Egyptians, and Pakistanis, all the nationalities at the Sarir camp, viewed America as weak because our leader could be forced from office by public opinion. Middle Eastern leaders were judged by how far they could flaunt their laws thus proving their strength. I was amazed how different our opinions were about something like a president being forced from office. I was proud to be an American, and I believe many of the critics probably agreed with me privately.

The Air Libya service was two DC-3s (see Figure 16) that made a least one stop at Sarir each week. It was quite an event. People went out to greet the plane for a social occasion. On Nov. 15, 1974, I wrote Linda describing the weekly plane, *"The plane circles the Sarir camp then lands on the sand runway. About 10 Land Rovers rush out to meet the plane. It's like a big impromptu party. People shake hands, greet the pilots and any newcomers, and look forward to the mail."* The pilots were American but were flying in Libya because their charter service had a tragic accident that their insurance didn't cover. They were working outside the US because money they earned would be forfeited for the unpaid damages. These were good guys and competent pilots. Their DC-3s were built in 1936 and they took them to Italy for regular serving and maintenance.

On a flight from Sarir to Benghazi, we asked the pilot to circle the infamous *Lady Be Good* so we could see this WW II American B-24 bomber. It had crashed April 4, 1943, when it overflew its base in Libya at night after an aborted bombing run to Italy. The pilots believed they could see waves in the Mediterranean Sea, but those waves were actually sand dunes in the Calanscio Sand Sea. The crew bailed out expecting to be rescued from the sea. The pilotless plane ran out of fuel and landed in the sand, but the men perished in the desert. Their remains were discovered in 1958 by a British Petroleum seismic crew who spotted a boot sticking out of the sand. At that time America had Wheelus Air Force Base near Tripoli. The human remains and parts of the plane were recovered by air force personnel but the plane, virtually intact, is still where it came down in the Calanscio Sand Sea.

On a flight from Sarir to Benghazi to meet Foster, a Bedouin family was on board. The DC-3s had five rows of seats up front with the rear area open for hauling equipment. Since this was a return flight the rear area was empty. The Bedouins built a charcoal fire on the metal floorboards of the DC-3 to brew their morning coffee. Smoke filled the cabin causing the co-pilot to run back from the cockpit to see where the smoke was coming from. Seeing the charcoal fire, he immediately got an extinguisher to put it out. No real damage was done but we had to breathe smoke until we landed in Benghazi. I doubt the Bedouins understood the words he said to them but I'm pretty sure they understood his meaning.

There were times when work was caught up and several of the engineering staff would decide to go exploring. Occasionally we would drive to the Sarir oil camp because there was a small shop that sold cheap imports from China such as work clothes, soap, toothbrushes, combs, pencils and paper, etc. I bought shorts that seemed more like culottes and a hairbrush and comb. I still have that comb and use it nearly every day.

Figure 1 — The Lebanese army barracks taken from Foster's west-facing apartment balcony. The exterior walls of this balcony had dozens of bullet strikes from gun fire between the Lebanese army and the PLO refugee camp (image by the author).

Figure 2 — The road into Foster's apartment from his north facing balcony where the PLO guards had their barricade. The refugee camp is to the right side. Downtown Beirut is in the background (image by the author).

Figure 3 — Forum of the ancient Roman Heliopolis Temple at Baalbek in the Beqaa Valley with snow covered mountains in background (image by the author).

Figure 4 — Large columns of the Roman Temple of Jupiter at Baalbek
(image by the author).

Figure 5 — The Temple of Bacchus at Baalbek. Beautifully preserved Roman Ruin.

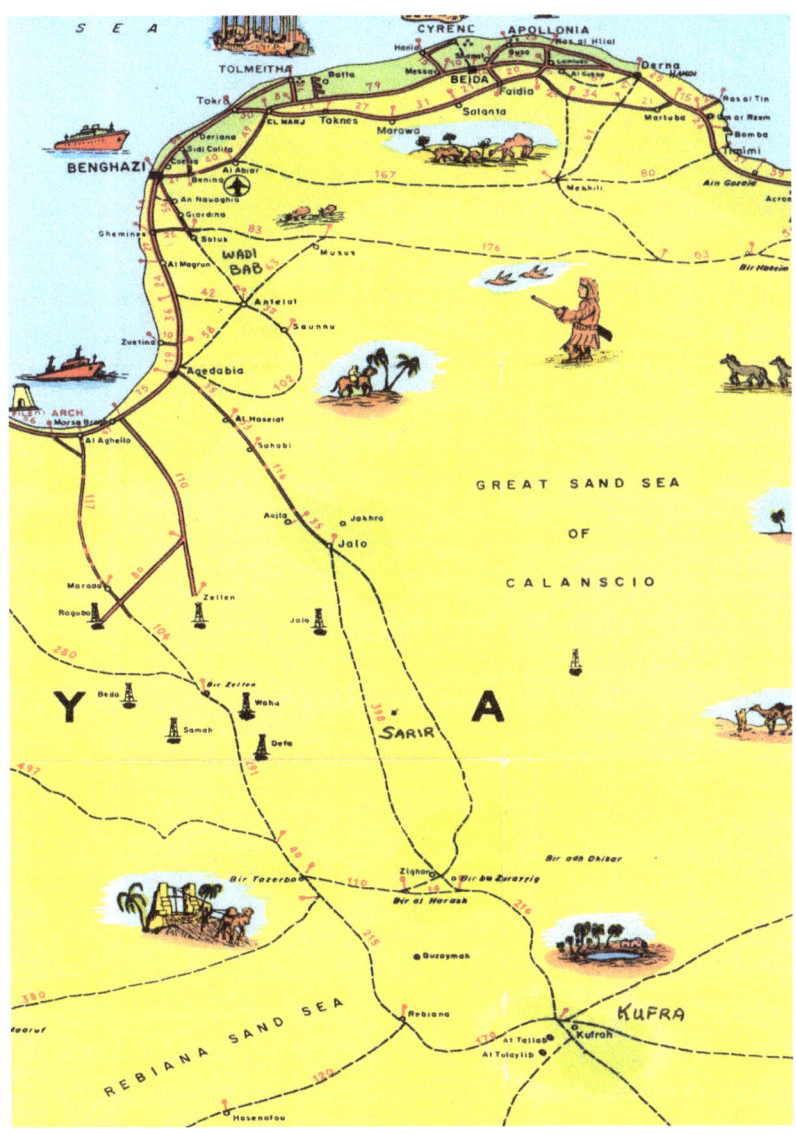

Figure 6 — A tourist map of Libya showing the route from Benghazi to Sarir and Al Jawf-Kufrah. It also shows the town of Ajadabeya where we stopped at the home of my driver to eat.

41

Figure 7 — We stopped at an abandoned fortress along the route to stretch our legs. I walked around and saw hundreds of spent rifle shells and debris such as boots and tin ware. I wondered if this was from the North Africa Campaign of WW II or some Previous war (image by the author).

Figure 8 — This is me standing by my Land Rover in front of my driver's home in Ajdabeya (image by the author).

Figure 9 — This picture was taken as we drove onto the sand and left the paved road heading into the Sahara Desert to the Sarir camp (image by the author).

Figure 10 — I drew this sketch of the Italian Road in my field notebook to show the typical markers on the road spaced one kilometer apart (drawing by the author).

Figure 11 — Seeing the sun disappearing into the desert sand was freaking me out having lost our water and fearing we would have to spend the night in the desert (image by the author).

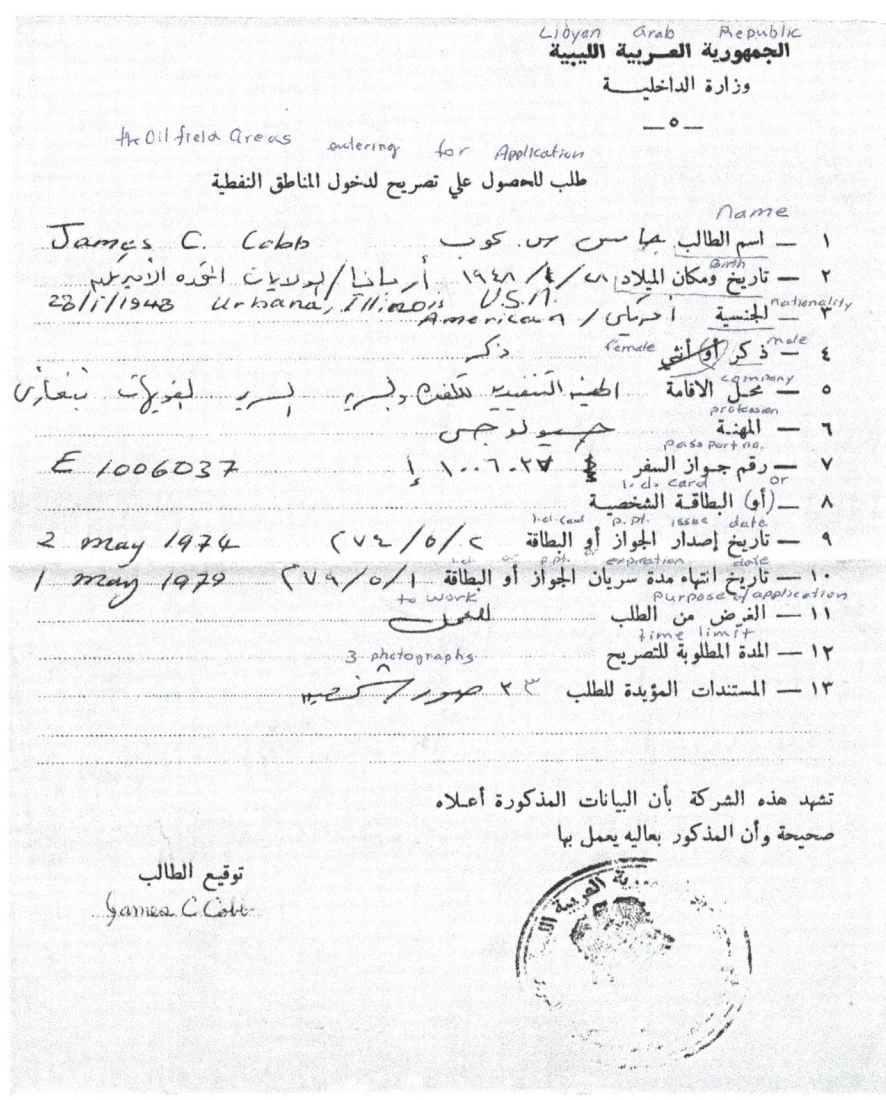

Figure 12 — My government permit allowing me to be in the restricted area of the Sarir oil field. The Sarir water project was close to the oil field so all workers for the water project needed one of these (image by the author).

Figure 13 — Sarir camp 1974 showing the dining facility, laundry, and camp power generator and fuel depot (background) but not the living quarters, repair shops, engineering office, equipment yard, or landing strip (image by the author).

Figure 14 — Three Failing 5,000 drill rigs at the Sarir camp that came overland from Kenya 4,000 miles to the south (image by the author).

Figure 15 — The senior staff at the Sarir camp in 1974 (I am fourth from left, image by the author).

Figure 16 — The Air Libya DC-3 at Sarir in 1974. It serviced Sarir camp and Al Jawf weekly (image by the author).

Figure 17 — Dunes in the Calanscio Sand Sea about 20 miles east of the Sarir camp. We enjoyed driving up these dunes for fun. Our Land Rovers were equipped with special sand tires for good traction in the sand (image by the author).

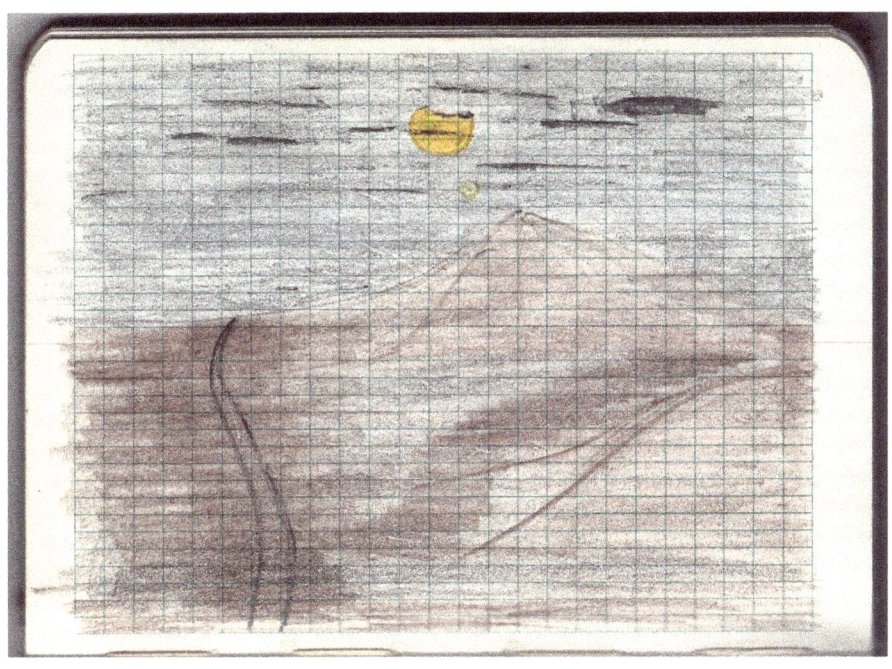

Figure 18 — This is my sketch of the Calancsio sand dunes I did in my field note book in 1974 (drawing by the author).

Figure 19 — My co-worker Fredrick Arthur Rawlings III inspecting an outcrop of limestone at Sarir. At least one of the vehicles at the Sarir camp had a bad accident caused by running into one of these outcrops at high speed that the driver did not see until too late to avoid it (image by the author).

Figure 20 — One of the drill rigs in operation at Sarir. It is an American made Failing 5000 model (image by the author)

Figure 21 — Geological staff at Sarir in 1974 (image by the author).

Figure 22 — I worked closely with crews on the rigs because I spent hours monitoring progress, taking samples, and running geophysical logs. The makeup of a typical crew was a Yugoslavian rig boss, Pakistani tool pushers, and Sudanese rough necks (image by the author).

Figure 23 — This shows the mud stream spewing out from the hose that carries cuttings from the well bore to the mud pit or brings samples from the well bore to be collected for study (image by the author).

Figure 24 — This is the Widco® 1200 geophysical logger being set up for logging a well at Sarir in 1974. The Widco® 1200 ran natural gamma, SP, and single point resistivity logs (image by the author).

Figure 25 — Surface geology exposed in a newly excavated mud pit. The profile shown in this image starting at the bottom is gray bioturbated silty mud, thinly laminated horizontal fine sand, inclined sand, thinly laminated horizontal fine sand, and on top loose white eolian sand. There is a pencil for scale (image by the author).

Figure 26 — Equipment for testing mud density at Sarir in 1974. Maintaining high mud density was vital because if it dropped too low the well would collapse causing loss of expensive equipment and the well itself. When the density was low, the rough necks would add bentonite from 80 pound bags until the density was raised to the safe level (image by the author).

Figure 27 — This image shows a pump test being conducted on a recently completed well in 1974. The test was used to determine hydraulic conductivity of the aquifer by recording drawn down in nearby wells installed for that purpose (image by the author).

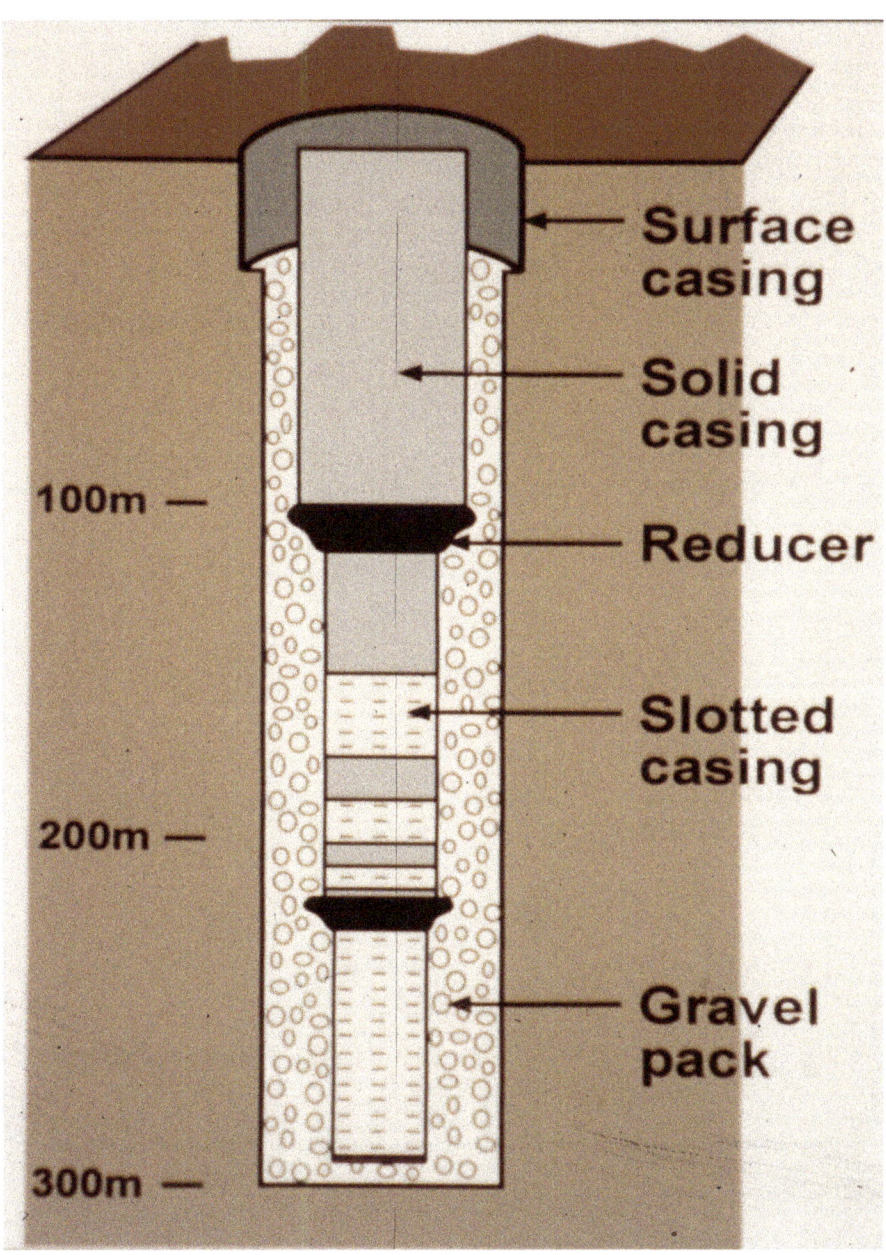

Figure 28 — This is a typical casing design for a well at Sarir in 1974. It shows solid casing, slotted casing, and reducers necking down the casing from 36 in., 28 in., and 18 in. (image by the author).

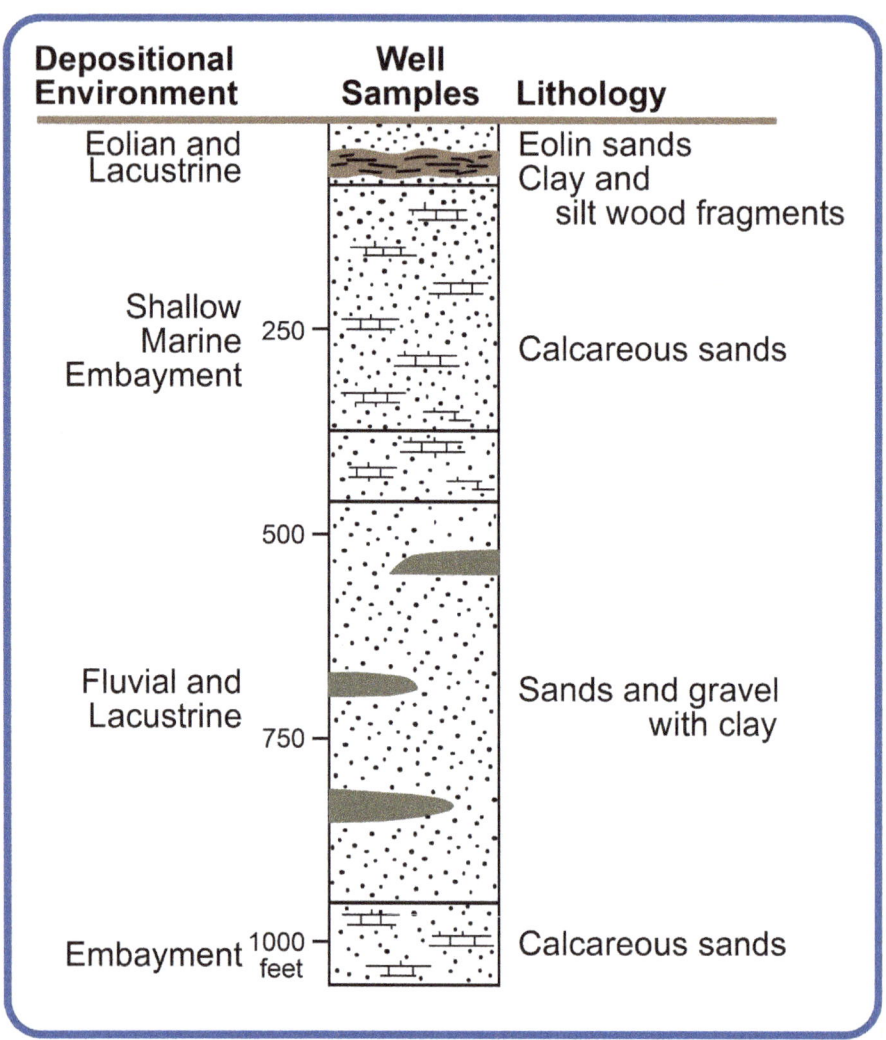

Figure 29 — My interpretation of the geology of the upper 1,000 feet at Sarir (drawing by the author).

Figure 30 — The first alfalfa crop in the background at Sarir in 1974 and the pivot irrigation machine (image by the author).

Figure 31 — The author on a break from the desert visited Zermatt and other places in Switzerland. This picture shows me with the Matterhorn in the background (image by the author).

Figure 32 — A recently dug pit being filled with drilling mud at Sarir in 1974. Two pits with drilling mud can be seen in the background. After drilling and casing were completed, these pits had to be reclaimed but if not done properly could be hazard (image by the author)

Figure 33 — Hastily made coffin for transporting the body of a driver who died after getting lost in the desert while driving from Benghazi to Sarir. The body is being returned to Benghazi (image by the author).

Figure 34 — Fly Mountain has been an important landmark for camel caravans near Al Jawf-Kufrah since ancient times (image by the author).

Figure 35 — This is me resting against one of the many highly oxidized Cambrian or Precambrian outcrops partially buried in recent sand. They are most likely erosional remnants of faulted and resistant older bedrock partially buried by younger sediments and exposed at the surface (image by the author).

Figure 36 — More Precambrian mesas in the vicinity of Al Jawf-Kufrah with operating pivot irrigators in the distant background (image by the author).

Figure 37 — Precambrian outcrops near Al Jawf-Kufrah (image by the author).

Figure 38 — Typical landscape in the vicinity of A1 Jawf-Kufrah (image by the author).

Figure 39 — Ancient ruins at Al Jawf-Kufrah with mesas in the background (image by the author).

Figure 40 — It was quite a surprise to see a camel caravan passing Al Jawf-Kufrah in 1975. I had been told that such caravans were a thing of the past and were no longer seen (image by the author).

Figure 41 — Oasis lake at Al Jawf-Kufrah (image by the author).

Figure 42 — Oasis lake at Al Jawf-Kufrah (image by the author).

Figure 43 — This pyramid shaped mound had vegetation growing in it but was also being covered by windblown sand. The water table was near enough to the surface to keep vegetation alive even while it is being buried (image by the author).

Figure 44 — A farmer and young girl at Al Jawf with their donkey. He kindly offered me fresh lettuce (image by the author).

Figure 45 — The Gearhart-Owen® 3200 geophysical logger I used at Al Jawf-Kufra. It was capable of natural gamma, SP, 16-64 resistivity, caliper, flow meter, temperature, and neutron logging and had 2,200 feet of four-conductor cable (image by the author).

Figure 46 — This shows the logging van set up to log at well at Al Jawf-Kufra in 1975. There is a tripod set up over the well bore to guide the cable with probe down the borehole (image by the author).

Figure 47 — Logging operations underway at a well at AI Jawf-Kufra in 1975. The logger was powered by a generator, seen on the left, so as not to overheat the truck engine (image by the author).

Figure 48 — Logging a well at AI Jawf-Kufra in 1975. The steel stand pipe from the well and tripod that guides the cable and probe down the well can be seen. The red globe on the right is for safe storage of the radioactive isotopes. It shields people from harmful radiation emitted by the isotopes used for neutron logging (image by the author).

Figure 49 — Sheep being fed alfalfa raised with the pivot irrigation machines at Al Jawf-Kufrah in 1975 (image by the author).

Figure 50 — Greek or Roman ruins at Apollonia-Cyrenaica in Libya in 1975 (image by the author).

Figure 51 — Greek or Roman ruins at Apollonia-Cyrenaica in Libya in 1975 (image by the author).

Figure 52 — The hillside at Cyrenaica is honeycombed with the Roman necropolis. There was a modern villa that we were told was used as a retreat by Mussolini (image by the author).

Figure 53 — This structure at Cyrenaica appears to be the remains of a Roman communal toilet facility. Only wooden toilet seats and a roof are missing but the plumbing system still had water flowing in it (image by the author).

Figure 54 — Marble floor at Cyrenaica still looks good after 2,000 years (image by the author).

Figure 55 — Ancient statue at Cyrenaica (image by the author)

Figure 56 — A 4th century earthquake caused devastating subsidence of Apollonia harbor. This structure carved out of rock now partly submerged appears to be a relic of Apollonia. (image by the author).

Figure 57 — Byzantine Christian temple possibly fourth or fifth century on the Libyan coast near Cyrenaica-Apollonia (image by the author).

Figure 58 — Marble column with the Byzantine Christian cross and globe at the temple (image by the author).

Figure 59 — Linda being a tourist in Rome in 1975 (image by the author).

Figure 60 — Linda when we first arrived by ferry boat from Naples to Capri (image by the author).

Figure 61 — Linda and me on the Isle of Capri. The two rocks in the far background are commonly photographed symbols of Capri (image by the author).

Figure 62 — Linda and me enjoying being the only people at the Villa Jovis palace built in 27 A.D. by Roman Emperor Tiberius. There is a path behind us leading to an overlook from which the drop to the sea is 1,000 feet down. Legends say Tiberius disposed of people who displeased him from this overlook (image by the author).

Figure 63 — Linda on a free beach in Capri, no sand only rocks. This is where I paddled out to the yacht Christina owned by Aristotle Onassis on my five-dollar raft I got as close as the anchor chain before being waved off (image by the author).

Figure 64 — International border crossing between Lebanon and Syria in 1975 (image by the author).

Figure 65 — This view is taken from the international border crossing between Lebanon and Syria in 1975. The mountain in the background is Mount Hermon and on the other side is Israel (image by the author).

Figure 66 — I took this image in the Umayyad Mosque in Damascus in 1975 (image by the author).

Figure 67 — A chapel in the Umayyad Mosque in Damascus that tradition says contains the head of John the Baptist (image by the author).

Figure 68 — View of the Umayyad Mosque through the inner courtyard in 1975 (image by the author).

Chapter 8

Geology of Sarir

The Sarir water project was in east central Libya on the edge of the Calanscio Sand Sea, a vast area of sand and dunes extending for thousands of square miles (see Figures 17 and 18). The dunes were aligned north-south like giant waves. The landscape at our site was flat with sand and pebbles on the surface and very prominent sand dunes more than 400 feet high about 25 miles east.

The word "sarir" is used in geologic descriptions to characterize a windblown surface where sand has been winnowed away producing a pebble pavement. The landscape was devoid of vegetation and there were few outcrops of bedrock. Partially concealed by the sand were ledges of limestone that were not easily seen and could cause great damage to vehicles traveling at high speed. These rock ledges stuck up only a few inches and were a few tens of feet across then disappeared (see Figure 19). The limestone was well cemented and had a ring to it. I thought it could be freshwater limestone from the Plio-Pleistocene wet period, but I had no fossil evidence to support my interpretation.

When the Geotehnika drill rigs were operational (see Figure 20), my job became a routine of driving to each rig every day to check progress and describe cuttings. My days started at the engineering office with geology and engineering staff. My work was important because it provided data such as top of water table; depth of saturation; clay and mud layers – aquitards; and porous granular beds – aquifers. The job was to estimate the groundwater resources, identify the type of aquifers, and determine pumping rates for irrigation. This was a tough job because actual data were so scarce. I got along well with everyone in the engineering department that included the geologists (see Figure 21) and people from four different countries. My best friend was Mohammed El Shazly Farag from Egypt with whom I am still in contact. Shazly was a life saver for me because of his friendly and humorous ways made me feel comfortable. There was a time when Qaddafi ordered all Egyptians out of Libya but fortunately that didn't happen. Thankfully it was only an empty threat. Many of Libya's professional and technical jobs were filled by educated Egyptians who ran the utilities, banks, hospitals, and other positions of vital importance. I heard many times that Libya could not have functioned without them.

It took about a week and a half for a rig to drill a pilot hole (see Figure 22) that I would log. Much of the time was in the setup and clean up because so much equipment was involved. When a pilot hole was completed, I would analyze the samples that were collected during the drilling. The rig would drill down 3 meters (about 10 feet) then circulate the mud to bring up the cuttings from that 3-meter zone. The samples would be brought to the surface by spinning the bit with no down pressure and increasing the mud circulation. The circulation hose would be disconnected and the mud with drill cuttings in it would be collected in buckets (see Figure 23). The mud was then poured through screens that collected the samples. Clean water was used to wash off the sticky mud so the rock fragments could be inspected using a hand lens. The drill pipe rotating at high speed could knock off pieces of the side wall from above the drill bit; therefore, I needed to keep in mind that some fragments might not be from the zone being sampled. As the drilling penetrated deeper the *caving* problem got worse. The fact that the drill was penetrating predominantly unconsolidated sediments further exacerbated this problem. The geophysical and penetration logs were a big help in sorting out true sample material from material falling from above.

When the drilling crew was ready for logging, I would get a knock at my trailer door informing me to take the logger out to the rig. Logging was a slow process because the instrument had to be lowered on a cable to the bottom of the 1,000-foot-deep hole; then electronics and recorder were switched on; and the instrument was raised at a slow but steady rate to create the geophysical log (see Figure 24). Things could go wrong such as running out of paper or ink and short circuits could developed in the cable or tool so sometimes logs had to be run a second or even third time. If everything went well, the operation took about four hours, if not, it could take as long as 24 hours. There was pressure to finish as quickly as possible because the project paid the drilling company stand-by time while I was on site doing the logging. I did most of the logging during the night. I had a theory that the senior staff who were day shift personnel made sure the night shift did the heavy work of pulling drill rods so that pilot holes were usually completed at night. After the pilot hole was drilled, larger diameter bits were used to ream the hole to a larger diameter before the 36-inch well casing was installed. It took a week to install well casing and clean the drilling mud out of the well. The design of each well was based on the samples, geophysical logs, and penetration rate log. By comparing logs north to south and east to west, geologic cross sections were made to interpret the geology.

The well casing was fiberglass and reduced in size going down from 36-inch diameter at the top; then reduced to 24 inches several hundred feet down the well, then 18 inches, and finally 10 inches to the bottom. The pebble pavement at Sarir provided an important resource because laborers raked up piles of gravel to use in well construction. What a strange sight to see men out in the desert sand with garden rakes making piles of gravel. Front-end loaders came along to make bigger piles from the smaller ones that were then loaded onto dump trucks. The gravel was used to fill the annulus (the space between the well casing and the sidewall of the borehole). The gravel acted as a filter to prevent sand and mud from entering the casing and clogging the pumps.

When rigs were set up for drilling, large pits were dug about 20 ft. by 10 ft. by 10 feet deep (see Figure 25). The near-surface profile exposed at the surface showed at least two cycles of dune building and wind scouring. We collected pieces of intact wood from several of these pits from about four feet below the surface. I was aware of the importance of carbon-14-age dating of pieces of ancient wood. This was a common practice in Pleistocene (Ice Age) deposits of Illinois, and I had collected Pleistocene wood for age dating during work on my master's thesis. The wood from the mud pits was sent to London for dating but I was never informed what those dates were. I guessed the wood was in the 8 to 12 thousand years old range corresponding to the north African wet period.

Drilling mud is a mixture of the mineral barite, bentonite clay, and chemical additives. Barite is a dense mineral and bentonite is a sticky clay. The barite is ground to a fine powder and mixed with the clay. When these are mixed with water, they make a heavy fluid that when circulated through the drill bit can carry rock fragments back to the surface and into the mud pit. The fragments settle out in the pit and the mud is re-circulated into the well. The mud is regularly tested (see Figure 26) to be sure its density was high enough to prevent the walls of the well from collapsing. If the density decreases due to mixing with groundwater, then bags of mud were added. It was extremely important to keep mud density high because the collapse of the well could trap the drill pipes and bit in the ground costing the company tens of thousands of dollars to replace plus the loss of the well. Mud was tested often, and new 80-pound bags of bentonite added often. When mixing the mud, the roughnecks would get coated in white dust taking on a ghost-like appearance. The dust dried out their skin so when the crankcase oil in the rigs and generators needed changing these guys would lay under the rig so the oil running out would cover their bodies. It was bathing in oil to replenish their skin.

Cleaning the drill mud out of the wells after the casing was installed was a lengthy process. The well would be pumped at a high rate to pull mud out of the well. Fresh water would be circulated in the well replacing the drill mud. The pump would be turned on raising a column of fresh water in the well, then turned off allowing the column to collapse back down the well. This "rocking affect" would scrub the mud cake off the side wall. A 1,000-foot column of water falling back down the well could shock the well removing the sticky mud. This process was repeated until the discharge water ran clear and could take a week to complete.

We performed a pump tests by pumping a well for a month at over 1,500 gallons per minute and measured draw down in two nearby observation wells (see Figure 27). Plotting the cone of depression was successful and from that, calculations could be made about the hydrology of the groundwater. The groundwater discharged from this test created lakes several acres in size. It was crystal clear fresh water so, *"what the heck, in 90-degree F heat, I dove in, but it felt like a polar bear plunge, and I exited as fast as I entered."* Being in 90-degree heat but 55-degree water and 5 percent humidity made the swimming experience not much fun. I didn't do that again. Our newly created lake attracted several species of birds that were fun to watch but where those birds came from was a mystery. At Al Jawf-Kufrah the pump tests attracted hyenas as well as interesting birds.

Calendar of Well Logging.
July 10, 1974 – Logged well A-100 (Sarir)
July 13, 1974 – made repairs to logging equipment (Sarir)
July 14 – 21, 1974 – field work dunes, calcrete, oil camp (Sarir)
July 22, 1974 – Sampled C-132E (Sarir)
July 26, 1974 – Logged A-30E (Sarir)
Aug. 5, 1974 – Sampled SPP (Sarir)
Aug. 14, 1974 – Logged C-110 (Sarir)
Aug. 23, 1974 – Logged C-112 (Sarir)
Aug. 24, 1974 – Logged PZ-1 (Sarir)
Aug. 28, 1974 – Maintenance on WIDCO® 1200 (Sarir)
Aug. 29, 1974 – Sampled PZ-2 & B-122P (Sarir)

Aug. 30, 1974 – Logged PZ-1 (Sarir)

Aug. 31, 1974 – Logged B-122P (Sarir)

Sep. 2, 1974 – Ran pump test on PZ-2 (Sarir)

Sep. 12, 1974 – Bedouin family arrived at camp with dead child (Sarir)

Sep 14, 1974 – Logged DE-2/P (Sarir)

Sep. 19-Oct. 1, 1974 – Vacation to Italy and Switzerland (Sarir)

Oct. 5, 1974 – Sampled DW-1/P (Sarir)

Oct. 6, 1974 – Logged DW-1/P (Sarir)

Oct. 8, 1974 – Re-logged DW-1/P (Sarir)

Oct. 13, 1974 – Logged DW-5/P (Sarir)

Oct. 17, 1974 – Logged DW-6/P (Sarir)

Oct. 18, 1974 – Sampled EW-1/P (Sarir)

Oct. 20, 1974 – Logged EW-1/P (Sarir)

Oct. 23-24, 1974 – Ran verticality survey and pump test on B-129 (Sarir)

Oct. 25, 1974 – Sampled B-113 (Sarir)

Oct. 28, 1974 – Big sand storm hit (Sarir)

Oct. 30, 1974 – Logged B-129 (Sarir)

Oct. 31, 1974 – Sampled EW-2/P (Sarir)

Nov. 1, 1974 – Logged EW-4/P (Sarir)

Nov. 5 & 6, 1974 – Search for lost vehicle (Sarir)

Nov. 8, 1974 – Geology EW-1&2&3 (Sarir)

Nov. 15, 1974 – Sampled EW-6/P (Sarir)

Nov. 16, 1974 – Logged EW-6/P (Sarir)

Nov. 18, 1974 – Logged EW-5/P (Sarir)

Nov. 22, 1974 – Sampled DW-3/P (Sarir

Nov. 24, 1974 – Logged DW-3/P (Sarir)

Nov. 27, 1974 – Logged EE-2//P (Sarir)

Dec. 7, 1974 – Samples FW-6/P (Sarir)

Dec. 8, 1974 – Logged FW-6/P (Sarir)

Jan. – July 1975 – 10 wells in Kufra

After logging approximately 30 wells, I took the logs to Beirut to discuss the results with John Foster and prepare our report for the Kufrah-Sarir Authority. Our principal job was designing wells that best fit the geology. The well designs (see Figure 28) didn't vary a lot because the geology was uniform well to well. We had official Foster and Associates folders and labels printed for each suite of logs and casing recommendations. These were then turned over to the Libyan officials according to our contract. Because there were no maps for Sarir well field but were desperately needed, Foster purchased large photo enlargements of Landsat I satellite images of Sarir. NASA's Landsat I imagery was a new thing in 1974 available to the public. These could serve as vital base maps for the project on which the wells could be plotted. These enlargements were 24 x 36 inches in size and rolled up in a map tube. I hand carried the tube with the images from Beirut to Benghazi. The Libyan customs personnel at the airport wanted to look at what was in the tube. I unrolled the satellite images for the customs agents, but they were unsure what they were looking at. I tried to explain what the images were even pointed out the smoke trails from flaring gas at the Sarir oil field. Tensions immediately escalated as the customs officials realized I was carrying images of the highly restricted oil field. I was put into a cell-like room and left there for three hours. There was no air conditioning, water, or toilet, and I had no idea what was happening. An agent came to interrogate me, so I tried to get across that I worked for the Kufrah-Sarir Authority and to contact them. I showed him my permit to work in the oil field and my guest pass for the Sarir oil camp. After talking to him an official from the project arrived about an hour later and I was released but they kept the satellite images. This is life in a third world country with suspicious, ignorant, and overzealous customs agents.

Geology at Sarir for the top 1,000 feet we were drilling was predominantly unconsolidated sand, gravel, and mud, with calcareous sandstone and limestone (see Figure 29). These sediments indicated deposition under low gradient and low energy conditions such as a shallow marine embayment and low gradient fluvial conditions. The sediments were most likely deposited by rivers emptying into a marine bay. The geophysical logs and samples showed the middle part of the 1,000-foot section was dominantly river sand and gravel, with mud accumulated on floodplains. Limestone and calcareous sandstone were interspersed with the sand and gravel showing that marine conditions dominated at times while terrestrial fluvial conditions dominated at other times. The ironstone and red and green muds indicated oxidizing conditions existed when sea level was low exposing the sediments to atmospheric conditions and oxidation. The entire section was low energy with low-gradient rivers flowing into a shallow marine bay. Occasionally sea level would rise drowning the rivers and depositing carbonates then decline allowing the rivers to build out into the bay. This interpretation fits with the location on the eastern side of the Sirte Embayment, a large geologic basin in the center of Libya that existed from Tertiary to Pleistocene times. The geology of Sarir was consistent with this location.

Geologists working in areas where no previous work had been done hope for one or more distinct layers in the subsurface that can be traced from one well to the next acting as a marker bed. The only markers in the subsurface at Sarir were the red and green clay layers. These layers were distinct enough to be marker beds, but such deposits are usually localized not laterally extensive over large areas. Each well had three clay layers 50 to 100 feet apart vertically equally spaced. The geologic question was were the clay layers continuous or lenses? This mattered hydrologically because if continuous then the sand and gravel aquifers might be confined and under pressure but if discontinuous lenses then the aquifers were unconfined. This was an important distinction to be made because accurate resource estimates depended on ascertaining the hydrologic characteristics of the aquifers. The aquifer was unconfined, and recharge could not be determined so pumping the wells was a mining process because the water was not being replenished. It was believed the groundwater was Ice Age water from the North African wet period about 10 thousand years ago.

As the initial wells were being completed along several arbitrary north-south lines, geologic and hydrologic data were being collected. The actual layout of the well field had not yet been decided. This was a big deal because 100 wells were planned, and the geometry of the well field would be important. A meeting was held with Geotehnika personnel, project engineering staff, and Authority ministers with Soviet advisors from Benghazi. This was the largest and most important meeting about the Sarir project. It included Libyan, Russian, Pakistani, Indian, Yugoslavian, Egyptian, Palestinian, and one American; and I was also the youngest person in the room by at least ten years. The official language for the meeting was English and I was the only native English speaker plus several of the nationalities represented were unfriendly toward the U.S. I thought to myself, *"how ironic is this."*

I had expected to sit in the back and just be an observer but as each question about the layout of the well field was discussed the group looked to me to validate the proposal before a final decision was made. I never thought that I would be put in that position especially since I was young and inexperienced. Based on the limited hydrologic data that had been collected to that point (I think I had collected most of it) the hydrologic gradient was from south to north so the wells would be aligned east to west one kilometers apart in two lines, also one kilometer apart, with the second line offset one half kilometer. The wells would then be in triangles with their center points one kilometer apart so that at some time in the future they could be combined as the water table dropped. The lines would be spaced two kilometers apart to minimize interference from one line to the next. The irony of the meeting is something I have thought about years later. About this time one of the first wells to be completed had been equipped with a pivot irrigation machine and the first alfalfa crop was growing fast (see Figure 30).

Chapter 9

Holiday in Switzerland

I worked straight through for seven months without a break, so F & A bought a ticket to Italy for me. I stayed a couple days in Rome eating great food and seeing the Coliseum and Roman Forum, but I really wanted to see Switzerland, so I went from Rome to Switzerland by train passing through the Simplon Tunnel the world's longest. In Switzerland the first stop was the Matterhorn (see Figure 31). Couldn't believe I was seeing the world's most recognizable mountain peak. I ate fondue and slept in a small cozy hotel. I slept 24 hours straight. Switzerland was so safe and comfortable I really spaced out. I think the stress of being in a hostile country in a hostile environment where I was the only American had gotten to me. I remember the cleaning lady coming into my room in the afternoon and poked me to see if I was alive. I had never slept like that in my life. I visited the Jungfrau and the Eiger. At the Eiger, I met an American Army officer stationed in Germany. We decided to climb the Eiger. From the base there are ladders and narrow trails with cable handholds up to a really cool mountainside pub. After that it would be technical climbing, so we planned to turn back once we reached the pub. A couple was climbing ahead of us, but she had slipped and broken her ankle. When we came upon them they were in real need of help. We spent our day helping them back down. After my two-week break I headed back to Benghazi and my work in the desert. I left alpine

Switzerland by train and made it all the way back to Sarir in one day. I realized just how badly I needed that break.

Chapter 10

U. N. Inspectors Come to Sarir

After half a dozen pivot irrigators were in operation and crops growing, officials from the UN Food and Agriculture Organization came to inspect the project. Three FAO officials all British came to see the progress on the project. Three inspectors arrived and they looked to me like carbon copies of Frederick Arthur Rawlings III dressed in tailored desert clothes and carrying swagger sticks and clipboards. If this had been a movie set, they would have been mocked for being clichés. Of special interest to them was site reclamation so that the planned crops would be successful. The inspectors first visited the most mature sites, those reclaimed first and already growing alfalfa. Alfalfa grows fast so these fields looked good. I was going along with my Geotehnika buddies to observe the visitors because we had few visitors, and this was entertainment for us.

Clean up and reclamation was needed after all the heavy equipment was gone. After drilling and installation of well casing were completed, the rig and all axillary equipment moved to another site. Mud pits were particularly difficult to reclaim because they were large and filled with "sticky" mud. The mud pits were dangerous because they were quicksand on steroids (see Figure 32). If anyone fell into it; it would be nearly impossible to get out. Geotehnika usually pumped some of the mud out of the pits and spread it out to dry and mix with sand. Then the pits were covered with sand. Time was needed for the mud to de-water and seep into the ground but that would be a long time due to the nature of the mud. It did not de-water quickly. When cleanup was finished all evidence that the pits ever existed was erased. But as we found out, just a few inches of sand covering the pits created a dangerous hidden hazard.

The inspectors asked to inspect a site most recently reclaimed. I am not sure anyone thought about the mud pits when one of the inspectors was walking out to inspect the recently prepared field. Just by chance he happened to walk on the narrow berm between two pits now invisible below several inches of sand. He took a step to his right and went down into the mud. His face showed shock and surprise. He was in up to his eyes; his mouth spitting out mud. He clawed and struggled until he gained his footing back on the berm but unfortunately attempting to get to safety he stepped off into the pit on the other side of the berm. Again, he sank up to his neck and clawed and struggled his way onto the berm. By this time Geotehnika staff recognized the layout of the concealed pits and carefully made their way along the berm to help the inspector back onto safe ground. He was in shock. He spent the night in the infirmary to monitor his blood pressure and was evacuated by plane the next morning. I must admit I forced myself to be sympathetic for this poor fellow but after my bad experience with Frederick, British men in tailor-made desert attire and haute' attitudes weren't eliciting my sympathies.

Chapter 11

American Engineers Lost in the Desert at Sarir

At the end of the first year at Sarir, plans for a permanent electricity generating station were moving forward. An American company was contracted to build the permanent power plant for the Sarir water project to power the pivot irrigation machines and pumps. The crude oil from the Sarir oil field was very high quality that could fuel a power station right out of the ground with no refining needed. We heard that three American engineers with a Libyan driver left Benghazi for the drive to Sarir much like I did when I first came to Sarir. Also like I did, they got lost but unfortunately rather than veering off course to the east and rescue in the oil field, they veered west into an area with little hope of getting help. It took six days to find them but too late because one in the party had died. The three Americans survived but the Libyan driver died. The Americans were arrested and charged with his death. The Libyan government claimed the Americans ganged up on the driver and denied him the remaining water, so they lived, and the driver died. The Americans claimed the driver couldn't stand suffering from thirst and drank radiator fluid out of desperation. We heard later that the Americans were released to go home. Geotehnika was asked to recover the body of the driver for the flight back to Benghazi. Geotehnika constructed a coffin to transport the body (see Figure 33).

Chapter 12

Field Work at Al Jawf-Kufrah

Because of our experience at the Sarir project, F & A was awarded a second contract to do well logging at the Kufrah water project. Al Kufrah is a large province in southeastern Libya whose principal village is Al Jawf. It is an ancient village located at the largest oasis in Libya. It was important in ancient times and as a watering station on the caravan route from east central Africa to the Mediterranean Sea and famous for its high-quality fruit dates. The Dodge pickup with camper top built in Beirut was transported by Greek freighter from Beirut to Benghazi. It was driven by project personnel from Benghazi to Sarir. I drove it the 400 miles from Sarir to Al Jawf with my Egyptian friend who spoke English and helped plan the trip with precautions like extra food, water, fuel, compass, and a Honda generator. We had a list of waypoints along the Italian Road that we checked off as we drove. A thin flat piece of wood about 6 inches square with an 8-inch-high metal rod sticking up vertically from the center was attached to the hood of the truck so the driver could see it. This was a sun compass. The sun shining on the rod cast a shadow on the wood which the driver could see. When the vehicle was aligned according to the correct compass reading, tape was placed on the wood where the shadow was. We would then drive keeping the shadow on the tape, thus the vehicle on the correct compass heading. After 15 to 20 minutes, we would hop out to use the compass away from the metal in the vehicle and realign the vehicle then re-tape the sun's shadow because the sun and its shadow move. The drive to Al Jawf-Kufrah was much more formidable because it was out of the area of the oil fields, less traveled, and chances for help from other vehicles less likely although we did pass a couple vehicles heading north. One of them was an open bed truck with camels tied down in the bed of the truck.

We stopped to eat at a tiny shack along the way that served food. It had only two items on the menu: rotisserie chicken and warm orange Fanta. The eating area was outside because there was no space inside, and the chance of rain was zero, they didn't need indoor seating. It had only a couple broken plastic chairs and tables. They weren't expecting a large crowd since there was no one around for hundreds of miles except for the few vehicles that passed by and there was no line and no counter. We had to wait while the cook chased down and dispatched the chicken, then cleaned, and cooked it. When the chicken was ready, the cook cut it in two on an ancient board that was probably never cleaned and literally handed us each a half; no plate, no napkins, and no utensils but it was the freshest chicken I had ever eaten. Flies attacked immediately so if you took a big breath, you inhaled flies up your nose. It was not a pleasant experience because of the flies but the chicken tasted good. This had to be one of the most remote places in the world where a traveler could get freshly cooked food. It made me think about ancient travelers and how they survived their journeys thousands of years ago. They survived because of places like this one. We made the trip to Al Jawf in about eleven hours. My earlier experience driving to Sarir taught me that serious planning and precautions were needed for trips of hundreds of miles across the Sahara Desert. Having a partner who could communicate was a big help.

One of our most welcome sights was "Fly Mountain" (see Figure 34) a dark colored rock mesa sticking more than one hundred feet out of the sand. It was a well-known landmark on the ancient caravan route. When we saw Fly Mountain, we knew we were close. The geology was complex because faulting and differential erosion created an interesting landscape of dark colored rock sticking up through light colored sand.

The area of Al Jawf-Kufrah was like Utah with mesas sticking up through the sand (see Figures 35, 36, and 37). The mesas were from just the size of a boulder to several hundred feet high. The landscape (see Figure 38) was fascinating with these mesas, oasis lakes, and palm trees. In our spare time we drove out to the mesas to climb around and explore caves. There were ancient ruins (see Figure 39) at Al Jawf.

Not far to the northeast across the Egyptian border, a cave in a mesa had pictographs of people swimming, giraffes, and hippopotamuses. It is known as the *cave of the swimmers* and was described in the book, The English Patient. Archeologists dated this to the North African Wet Period of 8,000 years ago when north Africa had a wet climate with lakes and rivers.

After I had been at the camp at Al Jawf for a few months, I was surprised to see a camel caravan of 40 camels driven by Bedouins passing by. People there said they were probably coming from Sudan or Chad and on their way north to coastal cities to sell their camels (see Figure 40). I had been told that camel caravans were a thing of the past and could be seen no more crossing the desert. But seeing the real thing was quite a thrill. Al Jawf was important because of the oasis (see Figures 41 and 42), the last opportunity to get water before the long dry journey north or to replenish water supplies after many days journey on their return to the south. I could imagine ancient camel caravans travelling through Al Jawf carrying trade products, slaves, and wild animals from central Africa to Rome and other destinations on the Mediterranean Sea.

The oasis lakes were several acres in size with clear blue water and white deposits along the water's edge I assumed was salt. Vegetation predominantly palm trees and grasses were growing around the lakes but very close to the lake. The landscape also had unusual pyramid shaped mounds of dead looking vegetation (see Figure 43) in them but still alive. They also appeared to be catching blowing sand but the vegetation was still able to access the water table just beneath the surface. There were small garden farms where the locals raised vegetables (see Figure 44). I observed raised water tanks perhaps twenty feet high and capable of holding several hundred gallons of water. I assumed the local farmers pumped groundwater into these tanks then watered their crops as needed. As the high-capacity pumps for the large alfalfa fields increased in number, the water table was declining. There were rumors that the declining water table was causing conflict between the locals and the government officials running the large-scale irrigation projects.

My job at Al Jawf was to log 2,000 feet deep wells. This project had several parts. One part was wells for pivot irrigators like Sarir but deeper and in hard bedrock. The other part was wells for irrigating farm plots. Each plot was pie shaped and one-eighth of the irrigated circle. These plots did not have pivot irrigators but movable irrigation pipes that had to be manually moved from one plot to the next. I met Australian sheep experts who had been in Al Jawf several years teaching sheep raising to the locals. Al Jawf had a large sheep population producing mutton and wool. The Australians were great because they played football Australian style, made home-made beer, and were fun people. One of them had built something like an ice boat except with wheels for sailing on the sand. It could go quite fast across the sand. They discovered a WW II ammunition dump at the base of one of the mesas and in it were live mortar shells in wooden crates. These guys carried shells one at a time up to the top of the mesa and then threw it off to see if it would explode. Most didn't but some did. I watched but did not participate in this activity.

I began logging operations at Al Jawf with the Gearhart-Owen® 3200 (see Figure 45) that was much more sophisticated than the Widco®1200 logger I used at Sarir. The GO 3200 had: 16-64 electrical resistivity, spontaneous potential, natural gamma, neutron, temperature, flow meter, and caliper. The wells at Kufrah were 2,000 feet deep. Logging the Kufrah boreholes took a full day sometimes two days (see Figure 46). Running the geophysical logs was my job (see Figure 47 and 48) but I had no responsibility for interpreting the geology. That job was with a German consulting company. I did not see well cuttings or cores. I did not get to keep the logs. The geology was much different than at Sarir. Whereas Field Work at Al Jawf-Kufrah 119 Sarir geology was unconsolidated sands gravels, mud, and carbonates; the wells at Al Jawf were in Nubian sandstone of Cretaceous age.

Neutron logging required loading the downhole probe with a radioactive isotope either americium-beryllium 241or radium 244. The radioactive isotopes were stored in a red globe that looked like an oversized basketball that shielded the radiation and kept us safe. When an isotope was needed, I had to retrieve it through a special hatch on the globe using a 4-feet-long tool that screwed into the isotope then the isotope could be safely transferred to the probe. When doing this procedure, I wore a lead-lined apron the same as X-ray technicians wear.

The Al Jawf-Kufrah project was a success raising sheep (see figure 49) on alfalfa from pivot irrigation, something Col. Qaddafi could show off to the world. Col. Qaddafi brought Soviet Foreign Minister Andre' Gromyko to Kufrah to show off his project. The caravan drove through the well field and stopped to see the pivot irrigators in operation. Some of the men got out to look around. I was logging a well nearby, so my truck was in the area. The men saw my van and walked over to see what I was doing. They were Russians. I shook hands with them, they all seemed friendly and amused to be meeting an American. Gromyko also went to the sheep pens and was shown sheep shearing being done by Australian sheep experts hired to tend the flocks. Gromyko and the Russians were friendly to all, shaking hands and smiling, but the uniformed Libyan guards stayed back. None of the Libyan officials got out to greet the workers. Raising sheep by that time had been successful but there were problems because shelters to protect the sheep from the intense sun had not yet been completed.

Kufrah was an interesting because there were many visitors coming to see the progress of the agricultural project. I encountered professors from Arizona State University studying the biology of the oasis. The German Water Group who were consultants and supplied pumps for the wells, collected beautiful pieces of petrified wood that had eroded out of the sandstone. When a cargo flight came in carrying new pumps, they loaded the fossil wood onto the empty plane. The plane was a Boing 707 so it could carry a lot of petrified wood. There were places that looked like the Petrified Forest National Park in Arizona. The regular Air Libya flights brought excitement to some staff members who were in the "know" which meant they could buy Johnnie Walker whiskey for one-hundred American dollars per bottle, very expensive at that time. The local authorities were running a smuggling operation. Near the end of my time there, there were rumblings from the locals about the falling water table. The landscape with oasis lakes, palm trees, and red colored mesas made Kufrah an interesting and beautiful place to work.

Al Jawf had an outdoor theater. It was a walk-in not a drive-in theater. I paid at the entrance and picked up a folding chair from a stack at the entrance. I noticed the people in front of me had two folding chairs. The people I was with told me I needed two chairs because one was to sit on and the other to put my feet on. This was necessary because scorpions came out when it got dark and everyone kept their feet up so a scorpion wouldn't crawl up their leg. I was told Al Jawf-Kufrah had deadly scorpions. I remember the movie *Westworld* starring Yul Brynner and James Brolin. It was about a cowboy-themed resort where real people could play gunslinger and have shootouts with humanoid robots. The robots were supposed to be programmed not to shoot the resort guests but of course that's not how things turned out. I wondered if the people watching thought America really had resorts with cowboy robots having shootouts.

On a trip back to Benghazi I met up with a couple British workers from Kufrah and together we planned a trip to Greek and Roman ruins east of Benghazi on the coast. Apollonia and Cyrene, founded in 631 B.C. were large cities in ancient times (see Figures 50 to 55). Apollonia built by the Greeks was a thriving commercial center. Later in Roman times, it served as the harbor for the Roman city of Cyrene. The New Testament tells that Simon of Cyrene carried the cross for Jesus for his crucifixion. There was no tour guide and no *keep off* signs. After a couple hours of exploring, a groundskeeper came up to us. He had pockets full of Roman coins, small ceramic dolls, glass vials and bottles he wanted to sell. Many walls, statues, marble columns, and marble floors were in relatively good condition for being more than 2,000 years old. Some structures showed minor modern repairs. The foundation blocks for the harbor of Apollonia are now below sea level (see Figure 56) due to destructive earthquakes which explains the strange structures just off the coast visible in the shallow sea water. The later Byzantine Christian temples are several meters above sea level, built on the debris of previous periods (see Figure 57). There was a modern villa overlooking the site that was reportedly used as a retreat by Mussolini.

I spent most of 1975 in Al Jawf-Kufrah that was the quintessential desert oasis and village.

Chapter 13

Meeting Linda in Rome

I had worked so many hours of overtime that F & A offered to buy a plane ticket for Linda to Rome. Her only travel experience had been car trips to a state park in Indiana so this would be her first time flying and first time traveling out of the US. We had kept up a good correspondence by mail and I was sure she was the one for me that my hopes were to marry her. She felt the same, so our plans were set to meet at the Rome airport then see the sights. We found the Hotel Tritone' close to the Spanish Steps. We had ten days. Linda was flying from Chicago via Frankfurt to Rome. I worried about her connecting flight in Frankfurt. I was overconfident about my own travel skills because I nearly missed my flight to Rome. I flew from Benghazi to Tripoli where there was a short layover and passengers could deplane to wait in the airport café. What I didn't know was that flights were not announced on the loudspeaker like every other airport in the world, so I was sitting in the café when my flight to Rome boarded and was ready for takeoff. Fortunately for me someone noticed I was not in my seat and a Middle East Airlines stewardess came to the waiting area to find me. Obviously, I hurried onto the plane and into my seat. I arrived before Linda so was able to meet her flight. We stayed at the Tritone Hotel near the Spanish Steps. It had an old-fashioned open brass elevator and a lovely rooftop veranda overlooking Rome (see Figure 59). We ate croissants and drank hot milk and coffee for breakfast. We had a great time exploring Rome, took a night carriage ride around the Roman Forum and Coliseum, ate in great restaurants, and went to Naples and Capri (see Figure 60).

We celebrated her 24th birthday at the Regina Cristina Hotel on Capri and got the maître d' to put a birthday candle in a cake which was not a tradition in Italy. Since they didn't have small candles, they stuck a full-size candle in the cake for us. Capri was wonderful, known as a destination for jet setters. We took the hydrofoil speed boat from Naples (see Figure 61). We visited the archeological ruins of the Villa Jovis built for the deranged Roman Emperor Tiberius in about 27 AD (see Figure 62). It was 1,000 feet above the sea and there was a place that traditions held he had people thrown off the cliff when they displeased him. Capri is literally split into two halves, Capri and Anacapri, divided by a geologic fault. Ana Capri is about 1,000 feet higher than Capri. One of our most unforgettable rides was on a three-wheeled vehicle that took us up the 1,000-foot elevation on a road overhanging the sea. We thought we would surely die. The touristy Capri beach cost money so we found a free beach (see Figure 63). A yacht was anchored offshore of that beach. We learned from the hotel it was the Christina, Aristotle Onassis' yacht. I bought a $5.00 blow up raft and took it to the beach and got the idea to paddle out to the yacht. When I got to the anchor chain and reached out to grab on, a uniformed steward looked down at me as if to say get away and waved me off. He looked serious so I retreated to the beach. That night we went to a night club and were dancing but then noticed it was a gay nightclub, so we danced ourselves out the door. Capri was known for hand painted tiles and we had one made with **The Cobbs** on it. It was ready just as we were departing Capri.

Chapter 14

My Exit from Libya

For my departure after two years of work, I was treated to a special flight by the Air Libya DC-3. I got a flight all to myself to Kufrah and Sarir to pick up my personal items. It was a big surprise to all the Yugoslavians to see the plane land unscheduled and only one passenger – me. I packed up my personal items from my trailer at Sarir and said goodbye to my co-workers in the engineering department and the Yugoslavian camp personnel I had spent more than a year with; then the plane took me to Kufrah where I did the same, then it was back to Benghazi. My last time at the Sarir Camp was a bit melancholy to say goodbye to Mr. Spiro Rajic, camp manager and Mr. Predrag Markovich, manager of drilling operations. They had been good friends to me and made me a part of camp life that allowed me privileges and respect from all the workers. I had good times with the Yugoslavians and even learned to play chess. They treated me very well. Mr. Hasnain and Mr. Salim were also good people, professional and knowledgeable about their work. One of my colleagues, a young man from Pakistan, died in a traffic accident on his way to Egypt. My best friend Shazly I would miss. I left him my textbooks. He made life good with his humor and personality.

So many thoughts but no regrets on leaving Libya for the last time because I knew I would not return. I would remember the good times and bad in the desert and Beirut but having seen that life, I knew it wasn't for me. Getting an exit visa for my departure for Beirut took several days and more than a few dinars in baksheesh to government officials that thankfully our Libyan agent did for me. Once that was done, I was off on a Middle East Airlines flight to Beirut. I was in Beirut two weeks finishing up geology reports and preparing logs to submit to the Kufrah-Sarir Authority. Then unexpectedly, I was needed to go to Damascus, Syria to meet clients F & A had a contract for geophysical work.

F & A's new job was with a Lebanese drilling company to log water wells for the Syrian army. The company had drilled ten wells, but none was yet logged. Their contract required logs to be run before payment would be made. A log is taken as proof the well was completed. The company was in a bad situation because it had expenses to cover amounting to several hundred thousand dollars but wasn't getting paid. Without our geophysical logs the Lebanese company could not get paid. The problem was we couldn't get new logging equipment shipped from the U.S. Foster asked me to meet with the owner of the drilling company. He was the son of a well-known Lebanese family. I hired a car and driver for the 70-mile road trip from Beirut to Damascus (see Figures 64 and 65) and I stayed at the Oriental Hotel in Damascus. Upon arriving, I had a free afternoon to visit the old souk where I bought gifts and toured the Great Mosque (see Figures 66, 67, and 68). The Mosque contains a shrine that tradition says contains the head of John the Baptist. The company owner and I had dinner that night which did not go well. He spoke perfect English and let me know how angry he was about our lack of work and the difficult position his company was in. He said to me, *"you are a nice young man and I do not blame you personally,"* and then he said, *"we do not sue like in the US but settle things the Lebanese way."* I knew he meant violence - we could expect a bomb or shooting at our office or car. He said, *"If I was you, I would leave Beirut."* I passed this message to John Foster This threat came when my leave for the US was due, so I knew I was leaving Beirut very soon.. I hoped the best for John Foster and a speedy peaceful resolution to the problem.

Just a couple days later, I treated myself to dinner at a nice restaurant on my last night in Beirut. The next morning, I would be headed to the airport for a flight to Amsterdam with a one-night stay then from Amsterdam to Chicago to Champaign, Illinois. I couldn't wait. I just experienced a very disturbing trip to Damascus, so I was on edge. I was mulling over the experiences of the past two years. I had had enough of that life. I was eating alone when a very nice-looking British couple came into the restaurant and sat at the table next to mine. The man excused himself and went to the restroom, so the woman started talking to me. She told me she and her husband had sailed their yacht from England and would be staying at their Beirut residence for a few months. She said that she and her husband enjoyed the company of other westerners and I would be welcome to go sailing with them. Sailing in the Mediterranean she said was wonderful. She invited me to their apartment after the meal to get better acquainted. She said their apartment was close, in walking distance. She said something to the affect her husband was very understanding about her male friends, and not a possessive person. She would be very happy if I got to know her better. Her *over-the-top* friendliness and suggestiveness put me on guard. Her husband had gone longer than normal for a trip to the restroom. I'm trying to process all this. I had just been to Damascus where our company was threatened with violence and now this woman was trying to coax me into leaving the restaurant to join them at their apartment. I was not going anywhere except back to my hotel so I could make my plane flight the next morning. I believed this was a set up for something sinister but of course didn't know what that was. This wasn't normal. I excused myself and left the restaurant and hurried back to my hotel.

I left Beirut for Amsterdam the next morning and arrived mid-afternoon. I took a taxi into the heart of Amsterdam and stayed at a nice hotel. There was time to walk around the city see the canals and sights and have dinner. After dinner I walked around the canal district and was shocked by the spaced-out drug users and open brothels where girls sat openly in the windows advertising themselves. This was certainly a different world and not what I expected. It was now nighttime, and I was approached by an Arab fellow who perhaps noticed my desert boots or just the fact I was walking alone. My mistake was using my limited Arabic greeting and allowing him to get too close to me that encouraged him even more. He walked along side of me for a while asking questions. I told him I was a geologist working in the Middle East on my way home for a break. He was overly friendly putting his arm around my shoulder like we were old friends. I realized later he was feeling for my wallet that was in the inside pocket of my sports jacket. It contained a check for $20,000, part of my take home pay for my work in Libya. He guided me toward an ally but by then I was figuring out he wasn't being friendly but steering me toward an alley when I saw a second guy waiting there in the dark. Now I knew I was being targeted just as he put his hands on me and grabbed for my wallet. The other guy now came out of the shadows to hold me while the first guy got my wallet. He got his hand inside my jacket and grabbed hold of the wallet, but it stuck in the pocket. My wallet was larger than a typical billfold and had a strap around it that caused it to catch in the pocket. When he couldn't get my wallet out, he stooped down to retrieve a knife in his boot. My fear and adrenaline came on full force. Seeing his head at about knee level I kicked him hard in the face and punched like a wild man at the other guy. I landed several good kicks and punches and broke free. I ran as fast as I could all the way back to the hotel, went to my room, packed my suitcase and although it was only 10:30 p.m., I sat up all night just waiting to get to the airport for the plane to Chicago.

In the past week, I had been threatened in Damascus, targeted for who knows what in Beirut, and mugged in Amsterdam. All that was too much for me. I couldn't wait to get home and enjoy normal life away for all the dangers and hazards I had experienced.

I arrived in Chicago in the early evening and went through customs then waited at the gate for the plane to Champaign, Illinois. By sheer coincidence Bob Bergstrom from the Illinois Geological Survey was also in the waiting area for the flight to Champaign. He was the person who introduced me to John Foster, had also worked with him in the Middle East, and was now chief of the Illinois Geological Survey. It was a nice reunion and I probably didn't stop talking about all the experiences I had had in the past two years. I arrived in Champaign and Linda was there to meet me.

Epilogue

I admit there are times in my life that I can't remember the everyday activities. Much of my college and high school lives are a blur but I remember the events in the Middle East in detail. My diaries for 1974 and 1975 plus the 28 letters I sent Linda give details about what was going on in my life. These reinforce and clarify my memories. My work experience in Libya helped build my confidence and my resume'. The Arab Oil Embargo in 1973-74 helped steer me into fossil fuels - coal geology and the U.S. response produced jobs that paved the way for my career. Conditions continued to deteriorate in Beirut after I left there in 1975. Just a year or so later John Foster left Beirut and returned to the U.S. and became a geology professor at Illinois State University (ISU). He started the hydrogeology program at the ISU Geological Sciences Department and retired in 1998. Sadly, he died soon after retiring. As a tribute to John, ISU began the John Foster Lecture Series in Hydrogeology. I was invited to give the inaugural lecture and spoke about our work in Libya. It was a nice occasion, and I was happy to talk about the hydrogeology of Kufrah and Sarir. John certainly deserved this tribute, and I was happy to be there to speak about his vision and work.

The water wells I helped create at Sarir and Kufrah were a prime target for photographs by space shuttle crews on many shuttle missions. The large green circles in the light brown Sahara sand made attractive targets for photography. A Trivial Pursuit question stated the Great Wall of China was the only man-made structure visible from space but that was debunked as not true. The answer should have been Jim's water wells because those big green circles really were visible from space.

I received a job offer in coal geology from the Illinois Geological Survey and decided to take the offer and pursue a PhD in coal geology. The work in the Middle East was a real career builder for me and the Arab Oil Embargo was a huge green light to pursue energy for my professional specialty. My Middle East experience helped propel my career because I had been given important responsibilities at a young age. My PhD in coal geology led me to the University of Kentucky (UK) in 1980. This was a time when coal supplied more than half the electrical energy in America and Kentucky was America's leading producer. I retired after 34 years at UK, the last 15 as adjunct professor, State Geologist of Kentucky, and director of the Kentucky Geological Survey which was a department of UK. Also, the experience of living and working in foreign countries made me long for a normal and settled life in America. Being married to Linda for 50 years has given us a wonderful life and our early travel experience sparked a lifelong interest in foreign travel. I had other extensive absences while doing geology work in China and Indonesia so the burden of keeping our homelife going was all on Linda. She did it well without complaint. We have a daughter Sarah and two beautiful granddaughters Mollie and Lily. Maybe they'll read this book some day and say, "I never knew grandpa did that!"

Acknowledgments

The author wants to thank Meg Smath, editor for the Kentucky Geological Survey at the University of Kentucky, for editing my manuscript and Patty Weber at the University Press of Kentucky, Publishing Services Center for formatting, layout, and cover design for this book. Their efforts are greatly appreciated.